REIMAGINING FAITH FORMATION
FOR THE 21ST CENTURY

JOHN ROBERTO

REIMAGINING FAITH FORMATION
FOR THE 21ST CENTURY

ENGAGING ALL AGES & GENERATIONS

 LifelongFaith Associates

Cover and book design: Hillspring Books, Inc.
Publishing consultant: Huff Publishing Associates, LLC

ISBN 978-0-9823031-6-0

Lifelong Faith Publications
LifelongFaith Associates
40 Brighton Road
Naugatuck, CT 06770
www.LifelongFaith.com

CONTENTS

Introduction   1

CHAPTER ONE
Interpreting the Challenges   5

CHAPTER TWO
Reimagining the Vision   31

CHAPTER THREE
Reimagining the Model   57

CHAPTER FOUR
Reimagining the Curriculum   83

CHAPTER FIVE
Reimagining the Resources   121

Assessment Tool and Online Resources   134

INTRODUCTION

What does it mean to *reimagine*? Dictionaries define it to "reinterpret imaginatively," "rethink," "imagine again or anew," "form a new conception of," or "recreate."

Reimagining Faith Formation for the 21st Century is true to these definitions. In this book I rethink and recreate faith formation for a twenty-first century world. In so doing, I am proposing a "new conception" of faith formation that is faithful to our continuing mission of making disciples and promoting lifelong growth in faith—designed for people in the twenty-first century.

I believe we are at the dawn of a revitalization of the church's educational and formational ministry. I believe we can embrace new approaches that provide faith formation for *all* ages and generations in our faith communities and out in the world. I believe we are blessed with new thinking about learning and faith formation, and an abundance of new resources and digital media and technologies that can transform the way we do faith formation.

This book is a proposal for what twenty-first century faith formation can look like. Much has been written about the challenges facing Christianity and faith formation. This book seeks to provide a way forward. It reflects a decade of my thinking and conceptualizing and innovating. It reflects what I am learning from churches that are embracing twenty-first century approaches.

This book is also a "how to" for faith formation: How to address big adaptive challenges facing churches and faith formation? How to reimagine faith formation with a vision that honors the past and is open to the future? How to build a new faith-forming ecosystem that supports faith transmission and growth? How to design new models with the best understandings and practices of learning and faith formation? How to engage all people—wherever they may be on their spiritual journey?

Chapter 1 explores four big adaptive challenges facing churches and faith formation to identify the need for a new faith-forming ecosystem and new models of faith formation. These four challenges include:

1. increasing diversity throughout American society in the length of the life-span, in generational identities, in family structures and marriage patterns, and in the ethnic makeup of America

2. rise of new digital technologies that are reshaping society, and the emergence of a connected, networked society

3. dramatic changes and increasing diversity in the religious beliefs, practices, and affiliation of Americans

4. decline in religious transmission from generation to generation

Chapter 2 presents a reimagined faith formation ecosystem for the twenty-first century. For more than one hundred years in the United States, Christian churches had a highly integrated religious ecosystem. It was comprised of multigenerational family faith practice and religious transmission at home; strong congregational community relationships and church life, especially participation in Sunday worship; weekly Sunday school for children and youth (and in many cases adults); and church groups (youth, men, women). Many Christian traditions relied heavily on the ethnic faith traditions of their people to transmit faith from generation to generation—at home and at church. *And* all of this was surrounded by a culture that explicitly or implicitly supported the Christian value system and practices.

There is no way to go back to this older ecosystem. The new ecosystem I propose incorporates five, essential, interconnected components:

1. intergenerational faith formation in the congregation

2. age-group and generational faith formation in a variety of physical places and online spaces

3. family faith formation at home

4. missional faith formation to the spiritual but not religious and the unaffiliated

5. online and digitally enabled faith formation

Chapter 3 presents a reimagined model of faith formation as a *network* of relationships, content, experiences, and resources—in physical places and online spaces. This networked model of faith formation is *lifelong*—each stage of life from birth to death—and *life-wide*—everywhere, anytime learning within a network of mentors, teachers, family, and peers. It provides a wide variety of engaging and interactive content and experiences in online and physical settings (home, congregation, community, world). It offers faith formation content and experiences to respond to the diverse religious and spiritual needs of people today—from the spiritually committed and engaged to the spiritual but not religious and the unaffiliated. It enables congregations to become centers for lifelong learning and faith growth for *all* people by utilizing the best of the new digital technologies to bring an abundance of meaningful and engaging faith-forming experiences—in the congregation and the world, and in a variety of media—to people of all ages.

Chapter 4 presents a reimagined understanding of faith formation curriculum as a lifelong journey of discipleship—a process of experiencing, learning, and practicing the Christian faith as we seek to follow Jesus and his way in today's world. I propose eight characteristics or features of a lifelong faith formation curriculum that reflect our continuing mission, the new faith formation ecosystem, and a contemporary approach to learning. This chapter includes a ten-step process for designing a curriculum that supports these features and is built on a network model of learning.

1. *Holistic:* envisioning Christian faith as a way of the head, the heart, and the hands—informing, forming, and transforming people in faith and identity.

2. *Comprehensive and balanced:* developed around the eight primary faith-forming processes that facilitate faith growth and incorporate essential knowledge and practices of the Christian faith: caring relationships; celebrating liturgical seasons; celebrating rituals and milestones; learning the Christian tradition and applying it to life; praying and spiritual formation; reading the Bible; serving people in need, working for justice, and caring for creation; and worshipping God with the faith community.

3. *Systemic:* providing a curriculum for the new faith-forming ecosystem—an intergenerational faith formation curriculum centered in church life and events, an age-group and generational faith formation curriculum, a family faith formation curriculum for the home, and a missional faith formation curriculum for the spiritual but not religious and the unaffiliated.

4. *Lifelong:* spanning ten decades of life and addressing the uniqueness of each stage of life.

5. *Contextual:* addressing the needs, hungers, interests, and concerns of people today and their unique spiritual and faith journeys by embracing an approach that moves from *life* to *faith* to *life*.

6. *Digitally enabled:* complementing the gathered community settings with online learning environments and utilizing the abundance of digital media and tools for learning and faith formation.

7. *Connected:* linking church life, age groups/generations, daily/home life, and online life through continuous faith formation—connecting participation in church life and events with daily/home life by using online content and connections *or* reaching people at home and in daily life with online faith formation content and experiences that connect to church life and events.

8. *Multi-platform:* delivered and conducted in multiple settings—self-directed, mentored, at home, in small groups, in large groups, church-wide, in the community and world—and in physical and online learning environments.

Chapter 5 reimagines the role of faith formation leader as a *curator*. In the new world of abundant resources, the role of the faith formation leader is shifting from *providing* religious content and programming to *curating* religious content and experiences for all ages. A faith formation curator is a trusted guide who continually finds, groups, organizes, and connects the best and most relevant content and resources on a specific subject to match the needs of a specific audience. This chapter describes the importance of curation and how to curate high-quality resources for faith formation using a four-step process:

1. research and organize resources

2. identify potential resources for the curriculum

3. evaluate resources

4. connect the resources to programming

Final thought. We are at the beginning of a journey toward twenty-first century faith formation. This book seeks to be a first word in what I believe will be a new era for faith formation. Yet beginnings can be fearful, letting go of old ways of thinking and acting can very difficult, and embracing innovation and experimentation can be challenging. But this is what is required of us today. If we are willing to embrace the opportunities in reimagining faith formation, we can make a real difference in the lives of children, youth, young adults, adults, families, and the whole congregation.

I would like to close with these words from Seth Godin, written a day after the death of Nelson Mandela. They are words of inspiration and motivation for all of us.

> Others can better write about Nelson Mandela's impact on the world stage, on how he stood up for the dignity of all people and on how he changed our world.
>
> For those that seek to make a change in the world, whether global or local, one lesson of his life is this:
> *You can.*
> You can make a difference.
> You can stand up to insurmountable forces.
> You can put up with far more than you think you can.
> Your lever is far longer than you imagine it is, if you choose to use it.
> If you don't require the journey to be easy or comfortable or safe, you can change the world.

(Seth Godin, "Legacy of Mandela," http://sethgodin.typepad.com/seths_blog/2013/12/ a-legacy-of-mandela.html)

CHAPTER 1

INTERPRETING THE CHALLENGES

We all know the world is changing around us. We experience it every day. Sometimes we embrace particular changes and innovations and integrate them into our daily lives. At other times we are confused, fearful, and overwhelmed by the pace and enormity of the changes and wonder what impact they will have on us, our family, our community, and our future.

Religious congregations and their leaders experience the same changing world and respond in similar fashion—embracing and integrating some changes while being confused, fearful, and overwhelmed by others.

Some congregations deny that the changes are really happening or affecting them and continue to do "business as usual." Many others respond by putting more energy and resources into "tried and true" programs or projects, developed in an earlier era, to address the changing world only to be disappointed and discouraged when they don't produce the desired results. A smaller group of congregations and their leaders decide to reimagine church life and faith formation in the new world, developing new initiatives and projects.

Faith formation is contextual—the models, approaches, resources, and technologies we use are suited to particular eras. The schooling model of education in the twentieth century became the dominant paradigm for church education as congregations organized Sunday school classes by grade level, in school-like settings, with textbooks developed for grade levels or age groups, in one-hour sessions organized around the school year calendar, and so on. Youth groups and adult education followed a similar pattern. Sunday school and its variations became the dominant paradigm for congregational education.

Faith formation is contextual—it relies on the surrounding ecology for support and reinforcement. The twentieth-century model assumed a supportive (multigenerational) family faith practice and socialization, a supportive church culture, and people's participation in church life, especially Sunday worship. It relied on a whole ecology of faith-forming people and activities to support the hourly programming. Many Christian churches relied on the ethnic faith traditions of their people to transmit faith from generation to generation—at home and church.

Consider this: If someone had been away from church for fifty years and walked into a typical church education program *today*, they might feel right at home: classes organized by age group, textbooks, small groups, and youth group; scheduled on a weekly basis between September and May; and held at a church facility. Except for schools, in what other setting would people feel so familiar and comfortable after a fifty-year absence? It seems that far too many congregations assume that the educational models inherited from an earlier era still address the real lives of people in the twenty-first century.

We need to ask ourselves: Are the twentieth-century models up to the challenge of the twenty-first century world and its people? Are these older forms of faith formation sustainable today? What would new forms of faith formation, suited to twenty-first century people and life, look like? How can we develop adaptive and innovative initiatives that address the new context and enable us to provide vibrant faith formation for all ages and all generations in the twenty-first century?

Churches today face a huge adaptive challenge in developing faith formation for the twenty-first century. One way to frame this adaptive challenge is to imagine what faith formation in a congregation would look like if we "started from scratch." What models and approaches would we use? What types of faith formation opportunities would we offer? When? For whom? Where? What resources would we need? What technologies would we use?

This first chapter sets the context for faith formation in the twenty-first century. At the beginning of the 2010s, the book *Faith Formation 2020: Designing the Future of Faith Formation* identified driving forces that would most directly impact the future of faith formation in Christian churches and the ability of churches to provide vibrant faith formation for all ages and generations. These included:

1. growing number of people who were religiously unaffiliated and spiritual but not religious

2. declining participation in Christian churches

3. increasing diversity and pluralism in American society

4. increasing influence of individualism on Christian identity and community life

5. changing patterns of marriage and family life

6. declining religious socialization

7.   increasing impact of digital media and web technologies

As we now enter the second half of the decade, it appears that each of these trends has increased in importance and actually accelerated in its impact.

This chapter builds on the work of *Faith Formation 2020* by focusing on four, interconnected and significant adaptive challenges facing churches and faith formation today and into the future:

1.   increasing diversity throughout American society in the length of the lifespan, in generational identities, in family structures and marriage patterns, and in the ethnic makeup of America

2.   rise of new digital technologies that are reshaping society and the emergence of a connected, networked society

3.   dramatic changes and increasing diversity in the religious beliefs, practices, and affiliation of Americans

4.   decline in religious transmission from generation to generation

This chapter describes each of these challenges, providing research and analysis and identifies questions to help us frame the adaptive challenges facing us. Responding to these four adaptive challenges will launch leaders on a journey of learning, discovery, innovation, and experimentation—all directed toward twenty-first century faith formation that helps all people develop a vibrant and life-transforming relationship with Jesus Christ. How congregations respond to these four challenges will, in large part, determine the future shape of church life in America. The rest of the book is devoted to developing approaches to address these major adaptive challenges and help faith formation for all ages and generations *thrive* in the twenty-first century.

CHALLENGE: INCREASING DIVERSITY IN AMERICAN SOCIETY

Very few congregations are designed to address heterogeneity—diverse populations of people. Most congregations were designed for a homogeneous world where people were more alike than different. In the past one hundred years, congregations have been built around a particular ethnic community, a particular neighborhood or geography, a particular demographic (such as families or a particular generation), and so on. Faith formation followed this example and designed programming that made assumptions about the people they were serving: children come from two-parent homes, with same-faith parents, who are practicing their faith and attending Sunday worship.

What happens when the social landscape changes? We are seeing the emergence of a ten-decade life-span, a five-generational society, an ethnically diverse society and church, ten family forms, and the decline of marriage. How well is congregational faith formation designed to address this new diversity? How many faith formation programs are based on outdated understandings of the people in their congregation and wider community?

The Ten-decade Life-span

We can now talk about a ten-decade perspective on the life-span. According to projections from the United States Census Bureau, the population ages sixty-five and older is expected to more than double between 2012 and 2060, from 43.1 million to 92.0 million, representing just over one in five US residents by the end of the period, up from one in seven today. Again according to the Census Bureau, in 2014 children ages 0–18 were 25 percent of the US population; adults ages 19–64 were 61 percent; and adults ages 65 and older were 14 percent.

The Five-generational Society

There are now at least five distinct generations in America: the builder (or silent) generation (born before 1946), the baby boomer generation (1946–1960/64), generation X (1961/64–1979), the millennial generation (1980–1999), and the iGeneration (2000–). Generations have unique and distinctive identities that can be described by their relationship to institutions, relationship to authority, family relationships, work-life balance, communication styles, technology usage, learning styles, religious expression, and more. For example, in a Pew Research survey on "What makes your generation unique?" the generations described several key features of their own generation, ranked in order starting with most important (Taylor, 34).

Silent/Builder	Baby Boomer	Generation X	Millennial
WW II/Depression	Work ethic	Technology use	Technology use
Smarter	Respectful	Work ethic	Music/pop culture
Honest	Values/morals	Conservative/ traditional	Liberal/tolerant
Work ethic	"Baby Boomers"	Smarter	Smarter
Values/morals	Smarter	Respectful	Clothes

But these differences don't make for conflict. In fact, most Americans do not see differences between generations as a source of friction. The generation gaps that do exist focus more on the differences in the use of technology and lifestyles.

An Ethnically Diverse Society and Church

The United States is fast becoming a plurality nation, which means that no ethnic group will be more than 50 percent of the population. According to the latest (2012) United States Census Bureau report, there will no longer be a majority group as the non-Hispanic white population decreases in number while still remaining the largest single group.

By 2060 the percentage of white alone (non-Hispanic) Americans will decline from 63 percent to 43 percent; Hispanic Americans will rise from 17 percent to 31 percent; the black Americans population will rise to 15 percent; and the Asian Americans population will rise to 8.2 percent. The number of two or more race Americans will rise from 2.4 percent to 6.4 percent.

In "Changing American Congregations" (2014) Mark Chaves reports that American congregations have become more ethnically diverse since 1998.

> A key point is that although the population of congregations has itself become somewhat more diverse—for example, 7.7 percent of churchgoers attended predominantly Hispanic congregations in 2012 compared to only 1.4 percent in 1986—there also is meaningful change within congregations. Congregations, especially predominantly white congregations, have become more internally diverse since 1998. . . . The percentage of people attending congregations in which no ethnic group constitutes at least 80 percent of the regular attendees increased from 15.3 percent in 1998 to 19.7 percent in 2012. This is a steady and notable increase in the percent of congregations in which no one group has an overwhelming majority of the people. . . .
>
> Today's predominantly white congregations are less predominantly white than they were in 1998. The percent of attendees in congregations with at least some Latinos, Asians, or African Americans has increased steadily since 1998. In 2012, clear majorities of churchgoers in predominantly white congregations were in congregations with at least some blacks (69 percent) or Hispanics (61.7 percent), and almost half (48 percent) were in congregations with at least some Asians (Chaves, 2014, 7).

Chavez cautions that 86 percent of American congregations (containing 80 percent of religious service attendees) remain overwhelmingly white or black or Hispanic or Asian or whatever. However, there is noticeable change in a more diverse direction.

Diverse Family Forms and the Decline of Marriage

There is an expanding understanding of what constitutes a family today and a corresponding growth in the variety of family structures in America—kindred families, and non-kindred "families" who live in shared households with a depth and intimacy of relationships and support. We can count at least ten kindred family forms:

1. married couple with children (original biological family)

2. married couple with children (blended family)

3. single parent with children

4. unmarried couple with children

5. unmarried couple without children

6. same-sex couple with children (married or unmarried)

7. same-sex couple without children (married or unmarried)

8. grandparents and parents with children

9. grandparents as primary caregivers of children

10. parents with single young adults living at home

Today, among 100 representative children, just 22 live in a married male-breadwinner family, compared to 23 living with a single mother (only half of whom have ever been married). There are 7 living with a parent who cohabits with an unmarried partner (a category too rare for the Census Bureau to consider counting in 1960) and 6 with either a single father (3) or with grandparents but no parents (3). The single largest group of children—34—live with dual-earner married parents, but that largest group is only a third of the total, so that it is really impossible to point to a "typical" family. Today there is no single family arrangement that encompasses the majority of children ("Five Facts about the Modern American Family," Pew Research Center).

The number of multigenerational households is rapidly increasing in American society. Today more than 51.4 million Americans of all ages—or about one in six—live in multigenerational households. There is also a rise in grandparents caring for grandchildren with 7 million grandparents living with a grandchild and approximately 3 million children being cared for primarily by that grandparent ("Five Facts about the Modern American Family," Pew Research Center).

There also have been dramatic changes in marriage in America. The median age at first marriage is now twenty-seven for women and twenty-nine for men. These are the highest ages in modern history. In 2013, 26 percent of people ages eighteen to thirty-two were married (in 1960 it was 65 percent).

Mothers are waiting longer to have children. Today an America woman, on average, is expected to have 1.9 children (as compared to 3.7 in 1960). More babies are born to unmarried mothers than even before: 41 percent of all births in 2011 (up from 5 percent in 1960).

In 1960, 72 percent of adults ages eighteen and older were married; by 2011 just 51 percent were. In 2012, one in five adults ages twenty-five and older (about 42 million people) had never been married.

Approximately half of all marriages are interfaith marriages. And the number of marriages in religious congregations continues to drop. As one example, between 2000 and 2012, weddings in the Catholic Church dropped by 40 percent, according to data from the Official Catholic Directory.

CHALLENGE: THE IMPACT
OF DIGITAL TECHNOLOGY

New digital technologies and media are reshaping society and creating the emergence of a connected, networked society. To no one's surprise, fully 95 percent of all teens ages twelve to seventeen were online in 2014. Perhaps surprising, is that 87 percent of American adults use the Internet, with near-saturation usage among those living in households earning $75,000 or more (99 percent), young adults ages eighteen to twenty-nine (97 percent), and those with college degrees (97 percent). Fully 68 percent of adults connect to the Internet with mobile devices like smartphones or tablet computers ("The Web at 25 in the U.S.," Pew Research).

The adoption of related technologies has also been extraordinary. Adult ownership of cell phones rose to 90 percent in 2014, and ownership of smartphones grew to 58 percent ("The Web at 25 in the U.S.," Pew Research).

Reflecting on twenty-five years of the Internet, Pew Research asked people for their overall judgment about the impact of the Internet, toting up all the pluses and minuses of connected life. The public's verdict is overwhelmingly positive: 90 percent of internet users say the Internet has been a good thing for them personally; 76 percent of internet users say the Internet has been a good thing for society ("The Web at 25 in the U.S.," Pew Research).

There is considerable debate about whether online communication—through email, messaging, or social media—has strengthened or weakened relationships. Internet users' own verdict is overwhelmingly positive when it comes to ties to their family and friends: 67 percent of internet users say their online communication with family and friends has generally strengthened those relationships ("The Web at 25 in the U.S.," Pew Research).

Technology has transformed our lives around digital networks. According to Lee Rainie and Barry Wellman, authors of *Networked: The New Social Operating System*, we are in the midst of a "triple revolution"—the rise of social networks, the personalized internet, and always-available mobile connectivity—that are coming together to shift people's social lives away from densely knit family, neighborhood, and group relationships toward more far-flung, less tight, more diverse personal networks.

The *Social Networks Revolution* provides opportunities for people to reach beyond the world of tightly knit groups; affords people more diversity in relationships and social worlds—as well as bridges to reach these new worlds and maneuverability to move among them.

The *Internet Revolution* gives people communications power and information-gathering capacities that dwarf those of the past, allowing people to become their own publishers and broadcasters and creating new methods for social networking.

The *Mobile Revolution* has fundamentally changed the relationship between information, time, and space. Information is now *portable*, *participatory*, and *personal*. More than two-thirds of American adults and more than 80 percent of millennials create content through social networking sites, other social media, and their various rankings, ratings, commenting, and remixing applications. In an environment where most are "publishers" and "broadcasters" and where powerful search technologies make it easy to find such content, people can easily locate and connect with others who share their tastes, lifestyles, political beliefs, spiritual practices, health conditions, hobbies, or professional quests.

Barry Wellman coined the term "networked individualism" to describe the way loose-knit networks of people—especially millennials—are overtaking more tight-knit groups and large hierarchical bureaucracies as the most prevalent relationship structure. In the world of networked individuals, it is the person who is the focus: not the family, not the work unit, not the neighborhood, and not the social group. Many meet their social, emotional, and economic needs by tapping into loosely knit networks of diverse associates rather than relying on tight connections to a relatively small number of core associates. This means that networked individuals can have a variety of social ties to count on but are less likely to have one surefire "home" group of protectors and observers.

People still value their neighbors, because living nearby remains important for everyday socializing and for dealing with emergencies large and small. Yet, neighbors are only 10 percent of people's significant ties.

CHALLENGE: CHANGING PATTERNS OF RELIGIOUS BELIEFS, PRACTICES, AND AFFILIATION

Patterns of Religiosity

Over the past two decades we have witnessed dramatic changes in the religiosity of American Christians, especially as evidenced in the increase in the number of people who are no longer affiliated with any religion. According to Pew Research this represents 20 percent of all Americans and 32 percent of those in their twenties and early thirties; the percentage continues to rise to 34 percent among the younger millennials in their early twenties.

The following graph by Tobin Grant and his colleagues reflects the decline in religiosity in the United States between 1952 and the present. Previous declines in religion pale in comparison. Over the past fifteen years, the drop in religiosity has been twice as great as the decline of the 1960s and 1970s. Tobin Grant and his colleagues have researched this massive change in American religion by using a computer algorithm to track more than four hundred survey results over the past sixty years: surveys on worship service attendance, membership in congregations, prayer, and feelings toward religion. The result is one measure that charts changes to religiosity through the years. (Note: The way to interpret the scale is to see changes between decades, e.g., the difference between the 1960s and the 1980s is a decline of 1.5 standard deviations, but the difference between the late 1990s and 2013 is about 3 standard deviations—providing evidence of rapid decline in religiosity, church attendance, and the importance of religion in people's lives.) Grant writes:

> The graph of this index tells the story of the rise and fall of religious activity. During the post-war, baby-booming 1950s, there was a revival of religion. Indeed, some at the time considered it a third great awakening. Then came the societal changes of the 1960s, which included a

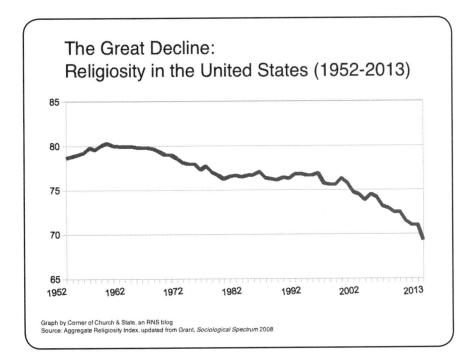

The Great Decline:
Religiosity in the United States (1952-2013)

Graph by Corner of Church & State, an RNS blog
Source: Aggregate Religiosity Index, updated from Grant, *Sociological Spectrum* 2008

questioning of religious institutions. The resulting decline in religion stopped by the end of the 1970s, when religiosity remained steady. Over the past fifteen years, however, religion has once again declined. But this decline is much sharper than the decline of 1960s and 1970s. Church attendance and prayer is less frequent. The number of people with no religion is growing. Fewer people say that religion is an important part of their lives.

Reinforcing this research is a 2014 study by the Barna Group on the unchurched population in the United States, drawing on more than two decades of tracking data. They found that nearly two-fifths of the nation's adults (38 percent) now qualify as post-Christian (as measured by fifteen different variables related to people's identity, beliefs, and behaviors). This includes 10 percent who qualify as highly post-Christian and another 28 percent as moderately post-Christian. There are generational differences—the younger the generation, the more post-Christian: 28 percent are elders; 35 percent are boomers; 40 percent are Gen Xers; and 48 percent are millennials. This helps to explain why America has experienced a surge in unchurched people—and why this predicts a continuing rise in this population.

Mark Chaves suggests that religious involvement has softened in part because American family and household structure has changed.

> The primary base for conventional, mainstream American religion remains the traditional family: people living in two-parent-plus-children households, along with older people who lived in such households until their grown children left home. Combining all the General Social Surveys from 1972 to 2008, married people with children at home are twice as likely to say that they attend services at least weekly as are divorced, separated, or never married people with no children: 32 percent to 16 percent. Childless married couples attend at rates closer to the non-married than the married with children: only 21 percent of these people say they attend weekly.
>
> The strong connection between family structure and religious involvement is important because the proportion of Americans living in traditional families, meaning two-parents-plus-children, has dramatically declined in recent decades. Compared to several decades ago, people now marry and have children later, more people do not marry at all, and married or not, more people remain childless. These are big changes.
>
> Religious involvement is softening because one of the most religiously involved demographic groups—married couples with children—is shrinking as a proportion of American society. Another demographic trend—more elderly people—may be a countervailing force, since older people also are among the most religiously involved segments of American society, but one of the reasons older people are more religious is because more of them

lived in traditional families when they were younger. As younger cohorts inexorably replace older cohorts, the elderly population will include more and more people who did not spend their adult years in traditional families and who did not attend religious services regularly. So the aging of the American population will help mitigate the softening of religious involvement for a while longer, but not forever (Chaves 2011, 52–53).

Chaves concludes by observing that fundamental and lasting change in American religious involvement is produced by demographic changes, especially changes in family and household patterns. "These demographic trends are where we should look for clues about the future of American religious involvement" (Chaves 2011, 54).

Diversity of Religiosity and Practices: Youth and Young Adults

From the National Study on Youth and Religion research studies we are discovering that diversity of religiosity and faith practices begins young—in adolescents and emerging adults (eighteen to twenty-five years old). In *A Faith of Their Own*, Lisa Pearce and Melinda Lundquist Denton examine three Cs of religiosity: the *content* of religious belief, the *conduct* of religious activity, and the *centrality* of religion to life. Understanding what a person believes, how a person practices his or her religion, and the extent to which religion is an important part of a person's identity provides a comprehensive sense of a person's religiosity. They identified five main profiles of adolescent religiosity. During the adolescent years 29 percent of teens are already unaffiliated (Avoiders and Atheists) and another 31 percent are minimally engaged (Assenters). (See Appendix 1 on page 26 for descriptions.)

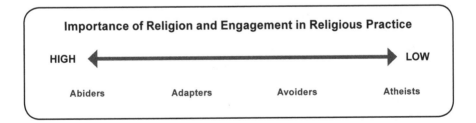

In *Souls in Transition*, Christian Smith and Patricia Snell continued their study of the same population who were adolescents in the *Soul Searching* and *A Faith of Their Own* books. They developed a typology of the different types of emerging adult religiosity. They believe that most emerging adults in America today fall into one of six different types when it comes to religion and spirituality. By the emerging adult years approximately 40 percent are not invested in religion—unaffiliated and not practicing, with another 15 percent are interested in spiritual matters but not committed. (See Appendix 1 on page 26 for descriptions.)

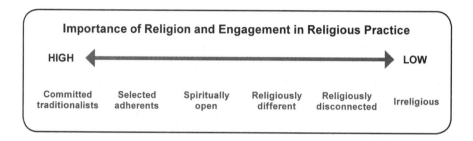

The Canadian study *Hemorrhaging Faith: Why & When Canadian Young Adults Are Leaving, Staying & Returning to the Church* identified four spiritual types that help to explain why some young adults still identify with and engage in church life and others do not. Only 23 percent of young adults are actively engaged in their faith communities. (See Appendix 1 on page 26 for descriptions.)

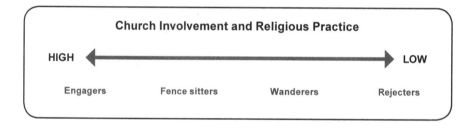

The Hemorrhaging Faith study found that churches were losing more young people between childhood and adolescence than between adolescence and the young adult years.

These three studies create a more nuanced portrait of the *content* of religious belief, the *conduct* of religious activity, and the *centrality* of religion to life in the lives of adolescents and young adults. The breadth of religious diversity as early as the high school years is having a huge impact on faith formation in the first third of life and focuses our attention on the effectiveness of religious transmission in the first decade of life.

The Rise of the Spiritual but Not Religious

The "spiritual but not religious" are the focus of news, conversations, and disagreements, but people who are spiritual but not religious are real people. They have disaffiliated from established denominational religion or religious communities.

Their spirituality is developed and lived out apart from traditional religious structures. The authority for their spirituality has been relocated *within*, relativized to each person, and detached from any particular spiritual community. Each person becomes his or her own spiritual authority.

In *Belief without Borders: Inside the Minds of the Spiritual but not Religious*, Linda Mercadante conducted in-depth interviews with a cross section of the Spiritual But Not Religious (SBNR). She found six common theological positions that were disavowed by the majority of her interviewees: "1) an exclusivism that rejects all religions but one's own; 2) a wrathful and/or interventionist God; 3) a static and permanent afterlife of glorious heaven and tortuous hell; 4) an oppressively authoritarian religious tradition; 5) a nonexperiential repressive religious community; and 6) a view of humans as born bad" (Mercadante 2014, 230).

Mercadante organized the SBNRs into five types:

1. *Dissenters* are people who largely stay away from institutional religion. Some are "protesting dissenters" who are hurt, offended, or angry with organized religion; while others "drifted dissenters," those who simply drift out of organized religion and never go back.

2. *Casuals* are people whose religious or spiritual practices are primarily functional, i.e., a given practice, teaching, or guide helps them feel better.

3. *Explorers* are like spiritual tourists who enjoy the journey but do not plan to settle anywhere. Some explorers occasionally attend traditional or alternative services. Theologically, they are hybrids, mixing and matching seemingly disparate beliefs, techniques, and spiritual practices.

4. *Seekers* are searching for a spiritual home. Some contemplate reclaiming earlier religious identities, moving on to something slightly different, or joining a completely new religion or alternative spiritual group.

5. *Immigrants* have moved to a new spiritual "land" and are trying to adjust to this new identity and community. Adopting a new religion requires commitment, constancy, and group loyalty, characteristics that vie with the SBNR ethos (independence, freedom, non-dogmatism, and an open and questing attitude). Many people could not take the strong disjunction from their native upbringing and eventually dropped out. "Surprisingly often, the source of their discomfort was theological. A religious or spiritual group often makes certain belief assumptions these newcomers found difficult to fully embrace, even with much effort" (Mercadante 2014, 64).

SBNRs present a huge challenge for established churches. Those that provide the basics of what SBNRs look for—informality, nonhierarchical leadership, recognition of diversity, deep participation—are more likely to be comfortable for

SBNRs. Mercadante reminds us of the theological concerns, "Unless the church takes seriously the theological reasons that they give for staying away from organized religion, any efforts to engage this population will be hampered. SBNRs represent an opportunity for churches to reinvigorate their ability to speak and think theologically" (Mercadante 2012, 33). She emphasizes the need for churches to address "four theological loci—the sacred (God), human nature (theological anthropology), community (ecclesiology), and the afterlife (eschatology)—and bring SBNRs' misperceptions and challenges out into the open" (Mercadante 2012, 33).

CHALLENGE: DECLINING RELIGIOUS TRANSMISSION FROM GENERATION TO GENERATION

The decline of religiosity and the increase in the diversity of religious belief and practice has resulted in declining participation in all aspects of church life—Sunday worship, marriages in the church, children and youth sacramental and ritual celebrations, children and youth programming. It has also resulted in declining levels of family religious transmission and faith practice at home. These trends are having a direct impact on developing Christian identity and a Christian way of life today.

Family religious transmission and socialization are the foundation for the development of faith and faith practices in children and for participation in church life and worship. As Christian Smith observes, "teenagers with seriously religious parents are more likely than those without such parents to have been trained in their lives to think, feel, believe, and act as serious religious believers, and that that training 'sticks' with them even when they leave home and enter emerging adulthood. Emerging adults who grew up with seriously religious parents are through socialization more likely (1) to have internalized their parents religious worldview, (2) to possess the practical religious know-how needed to live more highly religious lives, and (3) to embody the identity orientations and behavioral tendencies toward continuing to practice what they have been taught religiously" (Smith and Snell, 232).

Significant indicators, such as religious identification as a Christian, worship attendance, marriages and baptisms in the church, and changing generational patterns, point to a decline in family religious socialization across all denominations, but especially among Catholic and mainline traditions. Religious practice among the next generation of parents (young adults in their twenties and thirties) is especially influenced by marrying, settling down, having children, and raising them. Since individuals who marry are more likely to attend religious services than are those who delay marriage, the postponement of marriage and childbearing has contributed to the decline in church attendance. Complicating this picture is the fact that an ever-growing percentage of Christians (at least 30 percent) are not getting married in a religious ceremony. The less contact that young adults have with the Christian tradition through participation in a local church, the less family religious socialization that is likely to take place when they marry and have children.

We also see a decline in religious traditions and practices at home. There are a variety of reasons for this, such as the complexity and busyness of everyday life, but one of the major reasons is the religious literacy and religious experience of today's parents. Many parents did not grow up in families where they experienced religious traditions and practices. Many were away from a church for ten or more years before returning with their children for baptism or the start of Sunday school or first communion. They simply do not have the fluency with the Christian faith tradition or the confidence to share it with their children.

British researchers David Voas and Rodney Ling reinforce this picture as they describe how religious decline in Britain is generational:

> The gap between age groups arises not because individuals become more religiously committed as they get older, but because children are less religious than their parents. The results suggest that institutional religion in Britain now has a half-life of one generation, to borrow the terminology of radioactive decay. Two non-religious parents successfully transmit their lack of religion. Two religious parents have a roughly a 50/50 chance of passing on the faith. One religious parent does only half as well as two together. (As quoted in "Where Have All Believers Gone?" by Andrew Brown in *The Guardian*, September 16, 2009.)

If these trends continue, we will see less and less contact and involvement with Christian communities and the Christian way of life, and the continuing decline of religious transmission and faith practices at home.

The Importance of Religious Transmission

For almost four decades, Vern Bengston and his colleges have been conducting the largest-ever study of religion and family across generations. They have followed more than 350 families composed of more than 3,500 individuals whose lives span more than a century—the oldest was born in 1881, the youngest in 1988—to find out how religion is, or is not, passed down from one generation to the next. In *Families and Faith: How Religion Is Passed Down Across Generations*, Bengston and colleagues report their findings and propose a theory or model—*intergenerational religious momentum*—that integrates their research findings by identifying factors that they found encourage or impede intergenerational religious momentum (see the chart in Appendix 2 on page 29).

At the center of their findings and theory are *families*. They found that religious families are surprisingly successful at transmission. "A majority of the parents and young adults in our sample share similar religious identities, practices, and beliefs. For example six out of ten parents have young adult children who report they have the same religious traditions as their parents—or share their parents' preference for no affiliation at all" (Bengston, et al., 185).

They also found that parent influence on religious beliefs and practices has not declined since the 1970s. Following is a summary of their findings.

Parental warmth is the key to successful transmission. A high-quality parent-child relationship leads to higher religiosity. "It is the nature and quality of the relationship they have with their child that is crucial—perhaps as much or more than what parents do and teach religiously. Our study indicates that relationships with parents that are felt to be close, warm, and affirming are associated with higher religious transmission than are relationships perceived as cold, distant, or authoritarian—regardless of the level of parental piety. This is particularly true for relations with fathers" (Bengston, et al., 196). These warm, affirming relationships were most likely to result in the successful transmission of religion. Children and teens responded best to parents who were unconditionally supportive, who did not force their beliefs or practices on them.

Grandparents will have an increasing influence on religious transmission, support, and socialization in the twenty-first century. "About four in ten grandparents and grandchildren in our sample share the same religious tradition, while slightly less than this report the same frequency of religious service attendance and agreement on religious beliefs" (Bengston, et al., 187). Grandparents provide religious influence by replacing or substituting for parents' religious socialization—the "skipped generation" effect, and by reinforcing or accentuating parents' religious socialization.

Parents in a same-faith marriage help perpetuate religious continuity across generations. "This is most likely if there is a strong religious commitment, the partners regularly attend religious services together, and religion is highly salient in the lives of both partners. Moreover religion can strengthen same-faith marriages, leading in turn to more effective religious socialization of children in the family" (Bengston, et al., 187).

Interfaith marriage and divorce deter religious transmission. In interfaith marriages, where each spouse continues in his or her religious faith, the study found that the stronger the faith of one partner, the more likely the transmission of that faith. Divorce is often a disruptive factor in the transmission of religious tradition to children.

Religious "nones" are also products of intergenerational transmission. "In the 1970 survey one in seven unaffiliated young adult children had parents who professed no religious affiliation; thirty-five years later, in 2005, this increased to six in ten" (Bengston, et al., 187).

Generations differ in their perceptions of God and spirituality. First there was an increasing separation of religious practice from religious institutions over time. Second there was a growing differentiation between "religion," specifically organized religion, and "spirituality," meaning an internal, personal relationship with God. A third trend involved "the increasing complexity of religious and spiritual experience over time and the departure from the more clearly defined institutional boundaries of religion of the past by successive age groups" (Bengston, et al., 191).

Faith transmission is most definitely a family affair, but changes in the environment surrounding the family can have a huge impact. Bengston and his colleagues identify *Contextual Factors*—influences from contemporary culture, historical events, generational differences in religious expression—that can reinforce or detract from the intergenerational religious momentum and the probability of the child following in the parents' religious footsteps. There are also *Influences from Religious Organizations* that can reinforce or detract from religious transmission: congregational programs and worship activities, inputs from religious leaders, religious influences encountered in education, and the influence of friends on religious and practices.

The changes occurring in the contextual factors and in the influences from religious organizations are having a direct impact on the ability of the family (parents and grandparents) to transmit religious beliefs, practices, and way of life, and an overall decline in religious transmission. And the changes within the family—the rise of interfaith marriages, the impact of divorce, and the transmission of non-affiliation from generation to generation—are also major contributors toward the decline in religious transmission.

CONCLUSION

There is very little in our history over the past one hundred years that has prepared us for the challenges we now face. It is truly a new world! The enormity of these daunting challenges can make us fearful or, worse, lead us to deny their impact. Seth Godin, author, entrepreneur, marketer, and public speaker, provides us with wisdom on how to address the fear that these challenges can induce in us.

> "How do I get rid of the fear?"
> Alas, this is the wrong question.
> The only way to get rid of the fear is to stop doing things that might not work, to stop putting yourself out there, to stop doing work that matters.
> No, the right question is, "How do I dance with the fear?"
> Fear is not the enemy. Paralysis is the enemy.

Faith formation in the twenty-first century will need to create new models, approaches, resources, and tools to address the four big adaptive challenges described in this chapter. We will need an innovative spirit and a firm belief that we *can* provide lifelong faith formation for all ages and generations across a ten-decade life cycle; that we *can* address the changing patterns of America society (ethnic cultures, generations, families); that we *can* respond to the diverse religious beliefs and practices of people today; and that we *can* create new ways to promote religious transmission from generation to generation.

Works Cited

Bengston, Vern with Norella M. Putney and Susan Harris. *Families and Faith: How Religion Is Passed Down across Generations*. New York: Oxford University Press, 2013.

Brown, Andrew. "Where Have All Believers Gone?" *The Guardian*, September 16, 2009. (http://www.theguardian.com/commentisfree/andrewbrown/2009/dec/16/religion-unbelief-decline-british-christianity)

Chaves, Mark, and Shawna L. Anderson. "Changing American Congregations: Findings from the Third Wave of the National Congregations Study. *Journal for the Scientific Study of Religion*, 53: 676–686. (Available at: http://www.soc.duke.edu/natcong/Docs/Changing_American_Congs.pdf)

Chaves, Mark. *American Religion: Contemporary Trends*. Princeton: Princeton University Press, 2011.

"Current Population Survey." United States Census Bureau March 2014. (Henry J. Kaiser Family Foundation: http://kff.org/state-category/demographics-and-the-economy/population)

"Five Facts about the Modern American Family." Pew Research Center, April 30, 2014. (http://www.pewresearch.org/fact-tank/2014/04/30/5-facts-about-the-modern-american-family)

Godin, Seth. "How Do I Get Rid of the Fear." (http://sethgodin.typepad.com/seths_blog/2014/04/how-do-i-get-rid-of-the-fear.html)

"The Great Decline." Tobin Grant. Religion News Service, August 5, 2014. (http://tobingrant.religionnews.com/2014/08/05/the-great-decline-61-years-of-religion-religiosity-in-one-graph-2013-hits-a-new-low)

Mercadante, Linda. *Belief with Borders: Inside the Minds of the Spiritual but not Religious*. New York: Oxford University Press, 2014.

Mercadante, Linda. "The Seeker Next Door." *Christianity Today*, May 30, 2012.

Pearce, Lisa D., and Melinda Lundquist Denton. *A Faith of Their Own*. New York: Oxford University Press, 2011.

Penner, James, Rachael Harder, Erika Anderson, Bruno Desourcy, and Rick Hiemstra. *Hemorrhaging Faith: Why & When Canadian Young Adults Are Leaving, Staying & Returning to the Church*. EFC Youth and Young Adult Ministry Roundtable, 2012. (http://tgcfcanada.org/hemorrhagingfaith)

Rainie, Lee, and Barry Wellman. *Networked: The New Social Operating System*. Cambridge: MIT Press, 2012.

Roberto, John. *Faith Formation 2020: Designing the Future of Faith Formation*. Naugatuck, CT: LifelongFaith Associates, 2010.

Smith, Christian with Patricia Snell. *Souls in Transition: The Religious and Spiritual Lives of Emerging Adults*. New York: Oxford University Press, 2009.

Stiller, Karen. "Why They're Leaving." *Faith Today* (September/October 2012).

Taylor, Paul. *The Next America*. New York: Public Affairs, 2014.

"The Web at 25 in the U.S." Pew Research Center, February 27, 2014. (http://www.pewinternet.org/2014/02/27/the-web-at-25-in-the-u-s)

"Year in Review: Barna's Top 10 Findings from 2014." Barna Group. (https://www.barna.org/barna-update/faith-spirituality/701-year-in-review-barna-s-top-10-findings-from-2014)

REFLECTION AND APPLICATION QUESTIONS

Implications of the Research for Your Congregation

Use the following reflection questions to discuss the research presented in the chapter and imagine how your congregation can respond to the challenges.

Ten-decade Life-span

- How can your congregation embrace a ten–decade approach to faith formation?
- How can faith formation address the distinctive developmental needs and life tasks of each decade?
- How can your congregation respond to the growth in the 65+ population and the opportunities for ministry and faith formation?

Five Generations

- How can your congregation utilize a generational perspective in faith formation?
- How can faith formation address the distinctive identities and needs of each generation?

Ethnic Diversity

- How can your congregation involve multiple ethnic communities in the community's life and address their distinctive ethnic identities?

- How can faith formation engage the distinctive religious traditions and practices of each ethnic community?
- How can faith formation address the unique needs and life situations of people of ethnic communities?

Family Diversity

- How can your congregation connect with and involve the diversity of family forms in church life and ministries?
- How can faith formation address the diversity of family forms in programming and outreach? How can your congregation engage the whole family in faith formation?
- How does your congregation provide specialized programming and support for parents across the different family forms?
- How can your congregation develop a ministry with new married couples for support, enrichment, and faith formation?
- How can your congregation provide a continuity of ministry and faith formation from marriage through baptism into early childhood?

Digital Technologies

- What is the impact of the widespread adoption of digital technologies for congregational life and faith formation?
- How do you see the influence of the social networks, internet, and mobile revolutions in the lives of people in your congregation and the wider community?
- How can your congregation utilize the social networks, internet, and mobile revolutions in ministry and faith formation?
- What are the new opportunities in this new digital world?

Changing Patterns of Religious Beliefs, Practices, and Affiliation

- What will the trajectory toward increasing disaffiliation and declining religious practice mean for the future of churches and faith formation?
- How can you use the typology of youth and young adult religiosity to interpret their religious and spiritual needs?
- How can faith formation address the different types of religious profiles of youth and young adults?
- How can faith formation address the challenge of each religious profile from those with the highest levels of religiosity and practice to those who are indifferent and disconnected?

Religious Transmission

- How do you interpret the effectiveness of intergenerational religious transmission among the families in your congregation?
- How can your congregation provide a supportive community that nurtures and equips parents and grandparents to be faith formers who transmit the Christian faith?
- How can faith formation empower and equip families to develop a community of faith and practice at home that supports religious transmission?
- What needs to happen in your congregation and at home to support religious transmission and faith practice in the first decade of life?
- How can your congregation minister to mixed-faith parents and families experiencing divorce?

APPENDIX 1

Diversity of Religiosity and Practices: Youth and Young Adults

From the National Study on Youth and Religion research studies, we are discovering that diversity of religiosity and faith practices begins young—in adolescents and emerging adults (18–25 years old). In *A Faith of Their Own*, Lisa Pearce and Melinda Lundquist Denton examine three Cs of religiosity: the *content* of religious belief, the *conduct* of religious activity, and the *centrality* of religion to life. Understanding what a person believes, how a person practices his or her religion, and the extent to which religion is an important part of a person's identity provides a comprehensive sense of a person's religiosity. They identified five main profiles of adolescent religiosity. As you can see below, during the adolescent years 29 percent of teens are already unaffiliated (Avoiders and Atheists) and another 31 percent are minimally engaged (Assenters).

1. **Abiders** (20 percent) have highest levels of religiosity and practice.

2. **Adapters** (20 percent) have high levels of personal religiosity; attend religious services more sporadically.

3. **Assenters** (31 percent) believe in God and feel somewhat close to God, minimally engaged with their faith; and practice only occasionally.

4. **Avoiders** (24 percent) believe in God but have low levels of religious practice; often don't name a religious affiliation.

5. **Atheists** (5 percent) don't believe in God and don't attend services.

In *Souls in Transition*, Christian Smith and Patricia Snell continued their study of the same population who were adolescents in the *Soul Searching* and *A Faith of Their Own* books. They developed a typology of the different types of emerging adult religiosity. They believe that most emerging adults in America today fall into one of six different types when it comes to religion and spirituality. By the emerging adult years approximately 40 percent are not invested in religion—unaffiliated and not practicing, with another 15 percent interested in spiritual matters but not committed.

1. **Committed Traditionalists** (no more than 15 percent) embrace a strong religious faith, can articulate their beliefs reasonably well, and actively practice their faith.

2. **Selected Adherents** (about 30 percent) believe and perform certain aspects of their religious traditions but neglect and ignore others.

3. **Spiritually Open** (about 15 percent) are not very committed to a religious faith but are nonetheless receptive to and at least mildly interested in some spiritual or religious matters.

4. **Religiously Indifferent** (at least 25 percent) neither care to practice religion nor oppose it, and are not invested in religion.

5. **Religiously Disconnected** (no more than 5 percent) have little to no exposure or connection to religious people, ideas, or organizations.

6. **Irreligious** (no more than 10 percent) have skeptical attitudes about and make critical arguments against religion generally, rejecting the idea of a personal faith.

The Canadian study *Hemorrhaging Faith: Why & When Canadian Young Adults Are Leaving, Staying & Returning to the Church* identified four spiritual types that help to explain why some young adults still identify with and engage in church life and others do not.

1. **Engagers** (23 percent) are in church on Sunday. Almost all Engagers report having experienced God's love and answers to prayer. They are more likely to be female than male. Engagers generally report having opportunities to serve and lead in their local church and have attended Christian camps and mission trips. Their parents are most likely to have consistently lived out their faith at home and in a church context.

2. **Fence Sitters** (36 percent) attend church occasionally, but their attitudes toward church are still somewhat positive. Many have made life choices that conflict with the moral teaching of the church. They are likely to report having experienced God's love and answers to prayer, but also think it would be hypocritical for them to attend church. Most feel their church makes a positive difference in their community, but is not as accepting of people as it should be. They don't read their Bibles regularly, but many still pray. Their parents have likely been inconsistent in their patterns of church attendance and practice of spiritual disciplines. They may still want church, but on their own terms.

3. **Wanderers** (26 percent) have left the church building, but have not yet shaken the dust off their feet. Their parents are likely to have stopped attending church, thus bringing their own attendance to a halt. They find church moral teaching incompatible with their lifestyles and almost never attend. Wanderers think church has a positive role to play in society, just not in their lives. Prayer and Bible reading are almost completely absent from their lives. Those who hold onto their childhood religious identity usually do it for their families—the rest are likely to have written off organized religion. Wanderers, like most young adults raised as Christians, do not join other faiths.

4. **Rejecters** (15 percent) almost never darken the door of a church anymore. While they report having been raised Christian, half now say they are atheist and almost all have cut ties with organized religion. They are more likely to be male than female and report no experience of God's love or answers to prayer. Rejecters didn't have opportunities to use their gifts in church or to be involved in leadership. They are cynical about the motivations of Christians, reject Christian moral teachings, and find the church judgmental and unaccepting. The parents of most Rejecters never consistently lived out their Christian faith before their children. For Rejecters the church is out of touch, and attendance is pointless.

The *Hemorrhaging Faith* study found that churches were losing more young people between childhood and adolescence than between adolescence and the young adult years.

These three studies create a more nuanced portrait of the *content* of religious belief, the *conduct* of religious activity, and the *centrality* of religion to life in the lives of adolescents and young adults. The breadth of religious diversity as early as the high school years is having a huge impact on faith formation in the first third of life and focuses our attention on the effectiveness of religious transmission in the first decade of life.

Intergenerational Religious Momentum

Contextual Factors
- Influences from contemporary culture
- Influences from historical events
- Generational religious differences
- Religious influence of peers

Influences from Religious Organization
- Church, synagogue, temple activities
- Priests, ministers, rabbis, youth ministers
- Religious influences in school or college

Family Influences

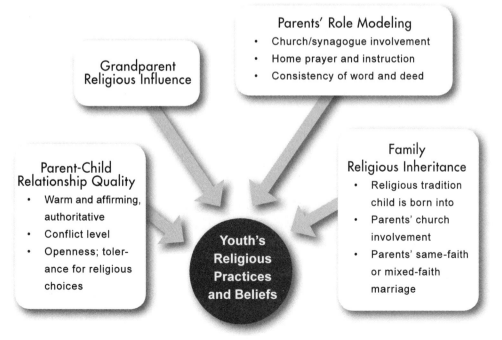

Parents' Role Modeling
- Church/synagogue involvement
- Home prayer and instruction
- Consistency of word and deed

Grandparent Religious Influence

Parent-Child Relationship Quality
- Warm and affirming, authoritative
- Conflict level
- Openness; tolerance for religious choices

Family Religious Inheritance
- Religious tradition child is born into
- Parents' church involvement
- Parents' same-faith or mixed-faith marriage

Youth's Religious Practices and Beliefs

CHAPTER 2

REIMAGINING THE VISION

You may recall the famous opening sequence to *Star Trek Next Generation* voiced by Captain Picard, "Space. . . . The final frontier. These are the voyages of the starship Enterprise. Its continuing mission, to explore strange new worlds. To seek out new life and new civilizations. To boldly go where no one has gone before."

This message captures perfectly the challenge for leaders in faith formation today. We need to embrace the continuing mission given to us by Jesus Christ: "Go therefore and make disciples of all nations, baptizing them in the name of the Father and of the Son and of the Holy Spirit, and teaching them to obey everything that I have commanded you. And remember, I am with you always, to the end of the age" (Matt. 28:19–20).

The goal of nurturing Christian faith in all ages and equipping people to live as disciples of Jesus Christ in the world has guided Christian churches for 2,000 years. "Christian faith formation is a lifelong journey with Christ, in Christ, and to Christ. Lifelong Christian faith formation is lifelong growth in the knowledge, service and love of God as followers of Christ and is informed by scripture, tradition and reason" (*The Charter for Lifelong Christian Formation*).

OUR CONTINUING MISSION:
MAKING DISCIPLES, FORMING FAITH

This robust, vital, and life-giving Christian faith is holistic: a way of the head, the heart, and the hands—informing, forming, and transforming people in Christian faith and identity.

- *A way of the head* (inform) demands a discipleship of faith seeking understanding and belief with personal conviction, sustained by study, reflecting, discerning and deciding, all toward spiritual wisdom for life. This requires that we educate people to know, understand, and embrace with personal conviction Christianity's core belief and values.
- *A way of the heart* (form) demands a discipleship of right relationships and right desires, community building, hospitality and inclusion, trust in God's love, and prayer and worship. This requires that we foster growth in people's identity through formation and the intentional socialization of Christian family and community.
- *A way of the hands* (transform) demands a discipleship of love, justice, peacemaking, simplicity, integrity, healing, and repentance. This requires that we foster in people an openness to a lifelong journey of conversion toward holiness and fullness of life for themselves and for the life of the world (see Groome, 111–119).

Congregations want Christian formation that *informs, forms,* and *transforms*; that immerses people into the practices and way of life of a tradition-bearing community where they can be transformed spiritually; and that engages all ages and generations in a lifelong process of growing, experiencing, celebrating, and living the Christian faith throughout life. While they may express this differently, Christian churches seek to help people:

- grow in their relationship with God throughout their lives
- live as disciples of Jesus Christ at home, in the workplace, in the community and the world
- make the Christian faith a way life
- develop an understanding of the Bible and their particular faith tradition
- deepen their spiritual life and practices
- engage in service and mission to the world
- live with moral integrity guided by Christian values and ethics
- relate the Christian faith to life today
- participate in the life and ministries of their faith community

Belonging—Behaving—Believing

How do we make disciples and form faith today? Most of us grew up with an approach that emphasized believing as the first step, then behavior, and finally belonging to a particular Christian tradition and community. Most of us are very familiar with this progression. Diana Butler Bass writes:

For the last few centuries, Western Christianity offered faith in a particular way. Catholics and Protestants taught that belief came first, behavior came next, and finally belonging resulted, depending on how you answered the first two questions. Churches turned this pattern into rituals of catechism, character formation, and Confirmation. At birth, Christian children were either baptized or dedicated, with sponsors and parents answering belief questions on their behalf, promising to teach them the faith. As children grew, Sunday schools and catechism classes taught Christian doctrine and the Bible, ensuring that each generation knew the intellectual content of the tradition. Eventually, children moved from Sunday school to "big church," where they participated in grown-up church practices and learned how to pray, worship, sing, give alms, and act kindly. When a Christian child reached an age of intellectual and moral accountability— somewhere between seven and fifteen—the church would offer a rite of full membership in the form of Communion, Confirmation, or (in the case of Baptists) adult-believers baptism. Believe, behave, belong. It is almost second nature for Western people to read the religious script this way (201).

This approach has led people to believe that religious commitment begins when one assents to a body of organized doctrines—and that this assent to beliefs, precedes and takes priority over behaving and belonging.

This pattern is changing. We are returning to a much earlier approach, grounded in Jesus' own ministry. "Long ago, before the last half millennium, Christians understood that faith was a matter of community first, practices second, and belief as a result of the first two" (Bass, 203).

Jesus begins his ministry with *belonging* by calling together a community—a community of disciples who were asked to leave everything and form a new community.

Jesus began with the inner life, the heart. Indeed, when he said, "You will know the truth, and truth will make you free," he was not speaking of a philosophical idea or set of doctrines. The truth is that the disposition of the heart was the ground of truth. Spiritual freedom results from a rightly directed heart, the self as it moves away from fear, hatred, isolation, and greed toward love. And, as Jesus also said, love is shaped through a relationship with God and neighbor, steeped in self-love and self-awareness. Faith, truth, freedom—all of it—is relational, not speculative (Bass, 205).

The early community that followed Jesus was a community of practice—a community of living the Way of Jesus (*behaving*).

They listened to stories that taught them how to act toward one another, what to do in the world. They healed people, offered hospitality, prayed together, challenged traditional practices and rituals, ministered to the sick, comforted the grieving, fasted, and forgave. These actions induced wonder, gave them courage, empowered hope, and opened up a new vision of God. By doing things together, they began to see differently (Bass, 207).

The beliefs that guide us as Christians are embedded in the community's life and the practices that give shape to that life and faith. Belonging and behaving lead to believing.

In the biblical pattern of faith, believing comes last. Indeed, this pattern repeats in both the Hebrew Bible and the Christian New Testament. From the calling of Abraham and Sarah through the great prophets and heroes of Israel to Jesus and the early church, those who walked with faith started by following, by becoming part of God's community, by enacting the practices of God's way, and finally by recognizing and proclaiming the glory of God (Bass, 209).

Relational community, intentional practice, and experiential belief are forming a new vision of what it means to make disciples and form faith in the twenty-first century. This perspective is woven throughout the vision of faith formation proposed in this chapter.

Faith-forming Processes

They devoted themselves to the apostles' teaching and fellowship, to the breaking of the bread and the prayers. Awe came upon everyone, because many wonders and signs were being done by the apostles. All who believed were together and had all things in common; they would sell their possessions and goods and distribute the proceeds to all, as any had need. Day by day, as they spent much time together in the temple, they broke bread at home and ate their food with glad and generous hearts, praising God and having the goodwill of all the people. And day by day the Lord added to their number those who were being saved (Acts 2:42–47).

We can discern at least *eight essential processes of forming faith*, informed by Scripture, theology, research, and contemporary reflection that promote faith growth and discipleship with age groups, families, and the whole faith community. The eight essential faith-forming processes—involving knowledge and practices of the Christian faith—facilitate faith growth *and* make a significant difference in the lives of children, youth, adults, and families. These eight faith-forming processes are central to Christian lifelong faith formation. They provide a foundation to address the challenge of religious transmission from generation to generation, and promote lifelong growth in faith and discipleship. The eight processes include:

- **Caring relationships.** Growing in faith and discipleship through caring relationships across generations and in a life-giving spiritual community of faith, hope, and love—in the congregation and family.
- **Celebrating the liturgical seasons.** Growing in faith and discipleship by experiencing the feasts and seasons of the church year as they tell the story of faith through the year in an organic and natural sequence of faith learning.
- **Celebrating rituals and milestones.** Growing in faith and discipleship by celebrating rituals, sacraments, and milestones that provide a way to experience God's love through significant moments in one's life journey and faith journey.
- **Reading the Bible.** Growing in faith and discipleship by encountering God in the Bible, and by studying and interpreting the Bible—its message, its meaning, and its application to life today.
- **Learning the Christian tradition and applying it to life.** Growing in faith and discipleship by learning the content of the tradition, reflecting upon that content, integrating it into one's faith life, applying it to life today, and living its meaning in the world.
- **Praying, devotions, and spiritual formation.** Growing in faith and discipleship through personal and communal prayer, and being formed by the spiritual disciplines.
- **Serving and justice.** Growing in faith and discipleship by living the Christian mission in the world—engaging in service to those in need, care for God's creation, and action and advocacy for justice.
- **Worshipping God.** Growing in faith and discipleship by worshipping God with the community of faith—praising God; giving thanks for God's creative and redemptive work in the world; bringing our human joys and dilemmas to God; experiencing God's living presence through Scripture, preaching, and Eucharist; and being sent forth on mission.

Writing about the educational imagination in congregational life, Charles Foster supports a view of developing proficiency in these types of processes. He writes, "An education that forms the faith of children and youth builds up and equips congregations (and their religious traditions) to be the body of Christ in the world" (126). This involves engaging young people (and their families, and all adults) in the disciplines of developing proficiency in the ecclesial practices of worshipping God and serving neighbor; involving them in the practices and perspectives, sensibilities and habits associated with being the body of Christ in ministry in the world; and preparing them to participate in and celebrate Christ's ministry as the focus of a congregation's education (Foster, 126).

It's important to remember that these eight processes are interconnected. For example: caring relationships flow through every process; worship has elements of reading the Bible, celebrating the liturgical seasons, and learning; celebrating rituals and milestones incorporate learning, prayer, reading the Bible, and worship. Maria Harris reinforces this point in her discussion of the church's educational ministry: "When we say the words of justice and do the work of justice, our speaking and doing are credible only if outreach and service are associated with the more inner-directed works of teaching, learning, and prayer. At the same time, outreach and service combined with prayer and study ensure that the work of justice will be informed and careful, based on solid thought, serious scholarship, and intelligent probing. They can make us strong in the head as well as in the heart" (Harris, 45).

These eight faith-forming processes provide essential elements for a congregation's comprehensive, lifelong plan for faith formation with age groups, families, and the whole faith community; and for family faith formation at home.

Faith-forming Processes in Research and the Christian Tradition

We see these eight faith-forming processes in research studies that give evidence to their power in forming faith with all ages and in families. For example, the research findings in *The Spirit and Culture of Youth Ministry* point to the power of the faith-forming processes within the congregation that develop maturity of faith in the lives of people.

- People experience God's living presence in community, at worship, through study, and in service.
- People learn who God is and come to know Jesus personally—learn how to be a Christian, how to discover the meaning of the Bible for their lives, and how to pray.
- People experience spiritually uplifting worship experiences that are enlightening, fulfilling, inspiring, interesting, easy to understand, and relevant in daily life.
- People develop moral responsibility—learning about Christian perspectives on moral questions and how to apply their faith to decisions about what's right and wrong.
- People are engaged in serving those who are in need, locally and globally.
- People experience a friendly, welcoming, and warm community life that provides love, support, and friendship.

We see these processes reflected in the Christian tradition. In discussing how parents can fulfill their central duties, Marcia Bunge identifies eight best practices often mentioned in the Christian tradition as ways to strengthen a child's moral and spiritual development:

1. reading and discussing the Bible and interpretations with children

2. participating in community worship, family rituals, and traditions of worship and prayer

3. introducing children to good examples and mentors

4. participating in service projects with parents or other caring adults and teaching financial responsibility

5. singing together and exposing children to the spiritual gifts of music and the arts

6. appreciating the natural world and cultivating a reverence for creation

7. educating children and helping them discern their vocations

8. fostering life-giving attitudes toward the body, sexuality, and marriage (Bunge, 14-18)

We see these processes reflected in Maria Harris's vision of the church's educational ministry, embodied and lived in five classical forms.

> Throughout history, reaching back to Acts 2:42–47, the church's educational ministry has been embodied and lived in five classical forms: *didache, koinonia, kerygma, diakonia, leiturgia.* If we would educate *to* all of these forms, as well as *through* all of them, then attending only to any one of them, simply would not do. The fullness of the pastoral vocation demands that any ecclesial education must be one that educates to:
>
> - koinonia (community and communion) by engaging in the forms of community and communion
> - leiturgia (worship and prayer) by engaging in the forms of prayer and worship and spirituality
> - kerygma (proclaiming the Word of God) by attention to and practicing and incarnating the kerygma, "Jesus is risen," in the speech of our own lives, especially the speech of advocacy
> - diakonia (service and outreach) by attending to our own service and reaching out to others, personally and communally, locally and globally
> - didache (teaching and learning) by attention to the most appropriate forms of teaching and learning in our own communities
>
> Should any of these be left out as full partners in the educational work of ministry; should any of these be downplayed; should any of these be exalted to the denigration of others, we will not be able to educate fully. All are needed (Harris 43–44).

We see these processes reflected in John Westerhoff's vision of a *community of faith—enculturation paradigm* in which Christian education uses every aspect of the church's life for education. "A viable paradigm or model for religious education needs to focus upon the radical nature of a Christian community where the tradition is faithfully transmitted through ritual and life, where persons as actors—thinking, feeling, willing, corporate selves—are nurtured and converted to radical faith, and where they are prepared and motivated for individual and corporate action in society on behalf of God's coming community" (45). Westerhoff identifies three aspects of community life around which we need to develop educational programs: "the rituals of the people; the experiences persons have within the community, and the actions members of the community perform, individually and corporately, in the world" (45).

These eight faith-forming processes are central to Christian lifelong faith formation. They provide a foundation to address the challenge of religious transmission from generation to generation and promote lifelong growth in faith and discipleship. They provide essential elements for a congregation's comprehensive, lifelong plan for faith formation with age groups, families, and the whole faith community; and for family faith formation at home.

These eight faith-forming processes are woven into each of the five elements of the new faith formation ecosystem proposed described in the next section.

Eight Faith-forming Processes

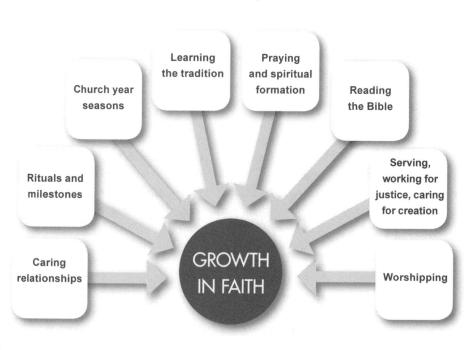

SEEK OUT, BOLDLY GO: FAITH FORMATION IN THE TWENTY-FIRST CENTURY

We need to be willing to seek out new, innovative approaches for faith formation that engage everyone—all ages and generations in all of their diversity—and to be willing *to act boldly* to bring those innovations to life. Faith formation in the twenty-first century will need to create new models, approaches, resources, and tools to address the four big adaptive challenges described in Chapter 1. We will need an innovative spirit and a firm belief that we *can* provide lifelong faith formation for all ages and generations across a ten-decade life cycle; that we *can* address the changing patterns of America society (ethnic cultures, generations, families); that we *can* respond to the diverse religious beliefs and practices of people today; and that we *can* create new ways to promote religious transmission from generation to generation. We are called to be faithful to the continuing mission of faith formation while at the same time creating new ways to live that mission in the twenty-first century.

A New Faith Formation Ecosystem

Among the most important tasks for twenty-first century faith formation is to create a new faith formation ecosystem for the continuing mission of making disciples and forming faith across the whole life span. What is an ecosystem? "An ecosystem is a system formed by the interaction of a community of living organisms with each other and their environment" (Dictionary.com). It is any system or network of interconnecting and interacting parts. As an example of interconnecting and interacting parts, think about Apple's "ecosystem" of hardware and software integration—how you can move seamlessly across Apple devices (computers, phones, tablets) using the same applications and accessing your content.

For more than one hundred years in the United States, Christian churches had a highly integrated religious ecosystem. It was comprised of multigenerational family faith practice and religious transmission at home; strong congregational community relationships and church life, especially participation in Sunday worship; weekly Sunday school for children and youth (and in many cases adults); and church groups (youth, men, women). Many Christian traditions relied heavily on the ethnic faith traditions of their people to transmit faith from generation to generation—at home and at church. *And* all of this was surrounded by an American culture that explicitly or implicitly supported the Christian value system and Christian practices.

There is no way to go back to this older ecosystem. As we saw in Chapter 1, this ecosystem has eroded over the past several decades because of all the changes in the culture and society, the family, technology and communication, and more. The environment has changed, and the relationship between congregational faith formation and its environment has changed. We need a new faith formation ecosystem that reflects this changed context.

The new faith formation ecosystem must be faithful to the continuing mission *and*, at the same, responsive to the challenges of the twenty-first century and the religious and spiritual needs of people today. This new ecosystem incorporates five, essential, interconnected components listed below and then explained in detail:

1. intergenerational faith formation in the congregation

2. age-group and generational faith formation in a variety of physical places and online spaces

3. family faith formation at home

4. missional faith formation to the spiritual but not religious and the unaffiliated

5. online and digitally enabled faith formation

The eight essential faith-forming processes (see page 38) are integrated into each of these components, providing both the processes for faith formation and the content—knowledge and practices of the Christian faith—of faith formation to facilitate growth in faith and discipleship in the lives of children, youth, adults, and families across the life cycle.

Intergenerational Faith Formation in the Congregation

Intergenerational faith formation and whole community faith experiences are at the *center* of the new faith formation ecosystem.

"Throughout Scripture there is a pervasive sense that all generations were typically present when faith communities gathered for worship, for celebration, for feasting, for praise, for encouragement, for reading of Scripture, in times of danger, and for support and service. . . . To experience authentic Christian community and reap the unique blessings of intergenerationality, the generations must be together regularly and often—infants to octogenarians" (Allen and Ross, 84).

This is the recognition that congregations themselves teach. People learn by participating in the life of a community. Practices of faith are taught through the interrelationships of worship, learning, service, ritual, prayer, and more. Among the events central to the Christian community are the feasts and seasons of the church year, Sunday worship and the lectionary, sacramental and ritual celebrations, holidays and holydays, works of justice and acts of service, times of prayer, spiritual traditions, and events that originate within the life and history of a individual congregation. A faith-forming education that is centered in the life of the Christian community is intrinsically an intergenerational experience.

Joyce Mercer, author and professor at Virginia Theological Seminary, asks the question this way: "What's the best curriculum for forming children and youth in Christian faith?" She responds by focusing on the formative power of the whole Christian community.

> *We invite people into the way of life that embodies God's love, justice, compassion, and reconciliation, by being, doing, and thinking about it together.* The best curriculum for forming children, youth, and anyone else in Christian faith is *guided participation in a community of practice* where people are vibrantly, passionately risking themselves together in lives of faith in a world crying out for the love of Christ.

> *Guided participation in a community of practice* puts a premium on both participation and practice. Watch children in play imitating the adults around them to see how even the youngest among us hunger to participate in the way of life they see enacted before them. That's a good instinct to follow, because people—children or otherwise!—don't become Christian by learning *about* what Christians do, say, or think (although at some point, particularly in adolescence and beyond, doing so can be an important part of deepening one's faith identity). We become Christian, taking on the identity of one who is a disciple of Jesus, by acting the way Christians act, and by talking the way Christians talk. Over time through practice, even our hearts and minds are formed in this way of life.

Mercer makes the point that guided participation in practice isn't just doing. It includes fully and actively practicing our faith in our everyday lives *and* making theological meaning out of the stuff of everyday life. In order to accomplish, we need places and ways to learn and inhabit faith stories.

Charles Foster writes, "A faith-forming education requires the interdependence of the generations" (128). This involves developing sustained patterns of intergenerational learning, relationships, and mentoring that develop young people's identification with the faith community, give them memories of hope to enliven their future, and create their sense of responsibility for the well-being of the community and the earth" (Foster 128–130).

Foster continues, "The responsibility of mentoring the faith of children and youth belongs to the whole congregation in the full range of its ministries" (131). This involves highlighting the community as mentor/teacher in which no one, yet everyone, may move in and out of the interplay of teaching and learning, of forming and being formed. The clearest way of learning to be Christian is to participate with others in the practices of being Christian. Each member of a faith community may potentially mentor someone at the threshold of expertise in some shared community practice (Foster, 131–132).

The research in *The Spirit and Culture of Youth Ministry* emphasizes the power of faith-forming congregational cultures where youth and parents come to know a living and active God through their relationships with God and the community. The young people in these congregations get to know Jesus Christ through the witness of believers and ongoing relationships with persons and communities who know Jesus. The power of faithful, multigenerational Christian relationships is at the heart of a congregational culture that develops and nurtures Christian faith in all ages and generations.

Most congregations are multigenerational by membership. Some are *intentionally* intergenerational. They make their intergenerational character a defining feature of their community life, ministries, and faith formation. These churches make it a priority to foster intergenerational relationships, faith sharing, and storytelling; to incorporate all generations in worship; to develop service projects that involve all ages; and to engage all generations in learning together. For these churches, being intergenerational is a way of life. It is an integral element of their culture. It is who they are!

Intergenerational faith formation and whole community faith experiences are at the *center* of the new faith formation ecosystem. Becoming intentionally inter-generational would:

- Form and deepen Christian identity and commitment as people develop relationships and actively participate in faith communities that teach, model, and live the Christian tradition and way of life.
- Provide a curriculum for the whole community—Sunday worship, the lectionary and church year seasons, learning, service, ritual and sacraments, prayer, and more—that is a shared experience in faith and belonging for everyone.
- Strengthen relationships, connections, and community across generations; enhance their sense of belonging in the faith community; and provide valuable adult role models for children and adolescents.
- Support families by surrounding them with a community of faith and engaging the whole family in a variety of faith-forming experiences together (caring relationships, celebrating, learning, praying, serving); and providing parents with opportunities to learn from Christians who are practicing their faith and raising faithful children.
- Strengthen the ability (confidence and competence) of parents and grand-parents to promote religious socialization at home; be role models of faithful practice; and engage in faith practices at home and develop warm, affirming, and unconditionally supporting relationships between parents (and grandparents) and their children, teens, and young adults.

Charles Foster writes, "A faith-forming education relevant to the challenges of contemporary experience engages congregations in the preparation of their children, youth, and adults to participate in the events central to their identity as Christian communities" (135). A faith-forming education centered on events includes the practices of *anticipation* through stories from the past associated with the event, of *preparation* in which we develop knowledge and skill for participating in the event, of *rehearsal* of event, of *participation* in the event, and of *critical reflection* upon our participation in the event (Foster, 135–141).

Among the events central to the Christian community are the feasts and seasons of the church year, Sunday worship and the lectionary, sacramental and ritual celebrations, acts of justice and service, prayer experiences, spiritual traditions, and the events that originate within the life and history of a individual congregation. A faith-forming education that is centered in the events of the Christian community is intrinsically an intergenerational experience.

Intergenerational learning provides people of all generations the opportunity to *prepare*—with the appropriate knowledge and practices—for participation in the central events of church life and the Christian faith and to *guide* their participation and reflection upon those events. In a variety of formats—large group and small group—intergenerational learning provides a variety of activities to address all ages: developmentally-appropriate, experiential, multisensory, and interactive.

Age-group and Generational Faith Formation

Age-group and generational faith formation address the unique life tasks, needs, interests, and spiritual journeys of age groups and generations across the whole lifespan. Intergenerational faith formation provides whole-community experiences and learning, focused on the central events of church life and the Christian faith, while age-group and generational faith formation addresses the unique needs of each stage of life. This provides a combination of intergenerational and peer-based learning and formation.

The eight faith-forming processes are a framework for an age-specific or generationally-specific curriculum. Instead of thinking of curriculum as content or themes, organized into sequential sessions and units by grade levels with textbooks, think of curriculum as the processes and practices that contribute to growth in faith and discipleship—a far more dynamic approach than a content-driven curriculum. Instead of thinking of classes and programs, think processes— how we guide people in living Christian lives today. The curriculum plan for each age group also includes "Life Issues" appropriate to that stage of life and "Discovering Faith" for initiatives to engage the "churchless" (spiritual but not religious and the unaffiliated and uninterested).

Intergenerational Faith Formation
and Age-group/Generational Faith Formation

Imagine an age-group curriculum designed around the eight faith-forming processes—each with developmentally-appropriate knowledge of the Bible and the Christian tradition, and experiential practice in the intergenerational faith community, at home, or as an age group. For example:

- People would learn about worship and how to worship; experience Sunday worship with the faith community and practice worshipping; and live the Sunday worship experience at home and in their daily lives.
- People would learn about the Bible and how to read it, interpret it, and apply it to their lives; experience the Bible at Sunday worship and at home; and develop their own practice of Bible study and reading.
- People would learn about Jesus and the Christian tradition—teachings, history, practices, what it means for life today, and how to live the Christian faith today; and experience the life of Jesus and the Christian tradition through participation in the events of church life, especially church year feasts and seasons.
- People would learn about prayer and spirituality and how to develop their spiritual lives through prayer and spiritual discipleship; experience the

prayer life of the faith community; and develop their own practice of prayer and the spiritual disciplines.

- People would learn about the justice issues of our day and the biblical and church teachings on justice, service, and care for creation; experience acts of justice and service with the faith community—locally and globally; and engage in the practices of serving those in need, caring for creation, and working for justice—as individuals, with their families, and with their church and other groups and organizations.

The age-specific curriculum engages people in the events of the intergenerational faith community—Sunday worship, the feasts and seasons of the church year, sacramental and ritual celebrations, works of justice and acts of service, prayer experiences, spiritual traditions, and events that originate within the life and history of a individual congregation—as integral to the curriculum.

Imagine a comprehensive, lifelong curriculum plan that is focused on the processes of growing in faith and discipleship that provides developmentally- and generationally-appropriate knowledge and practices; engages people intergenerationally in the life and events of the Christian community; and provides a focus for designing new programs and activities, as well as redesigning current programming, around faith-forming processes.

Family Faith Formation

The family is the single most important influence on religious transmission and faith practice—a truth demonstrated in research studies, the Christian tradition, and pastoral experience.

The reports from the National Study on Youth and Religion clearly show that the faith of parents and grandparents, their role modeling, and their teaching—both formal and informal, verbal and nonverbal, oral and behavioral, intentional and unconscious—are the key factors in developing highly religious children, youth, and emerging adults.

From the *Families and Faith* research (Vern Bengston, et al.) we learned that religious families are surprisingly successful at transmission (six out of ten parents have young adult children who report they have the same religious traditions as their parents) and that parental influence on religious beliefs and practices has not declined since the 1970s. We also learned that parental warmth is the key to successful transmission: a high-quality parent-child relationship leads to higher religiosity as demonstrated by the finding that parents who are felt by their children to be close, warm, and affirming are associated with higher religious transmission than are relationships perceived as cold, distant, or authoritarian. And we learned that grandparents will have an increasing influence on religious transmission, support, and socialization in the twenty-first century. Grandparents provide religious influence by replacing or substituting for parents' religious socialization—the "skipped generation" effect, and by reinforcing or accentuating parents' religious socialization.

Congregations need to equip families as centers of faith formation. Intergenerational faith formation and participation in church life can become a laboratory for immersing parents, grandparents, and the whole family in the Christian tradition, Christian practices, and Christian way of life. Participation in intergenerational experiences helps to develop the faith of parents and grandparents and increases their confidence and competence for engaging in faith practices at home. Intergenerational participation creates a shared experienced—often missing from everyday life—of families learning together, sharing faith, praying together, serving, and celebrating rituals and traditions. Families learn the knowledge and skills for sharing faith, celebrating traditions, and practicing the Christian faith at home and in the world; and they receive encouragement for continued family faith practice at home. Congregations can then provide resources to help families share, celebrate, and practice their faith at home through the new digital technologies and media.

The family component of the twenty-first century faith formation ecosystem has three "curriculum" areas:

- nurturing family faith and developing the faith life of parents and grandparents
- strengthening family life by focusing on family asset-building
- developing the knowledge, skills, and confidence of parents (and grandparents) for parenting

A curriculum for family faith formation utilizes the eight faith-forming processes as a framework for organizing knowledge, experiences, practices, and resources to nurture family faith and develop the faith life of parents and grandparents. First, we can focus on the whole family and design the eight faith-forming processes—with activities, practices, and resources—so that they can be embedded into the daily life of families. Sociologist Robert Wuthnow makes this same point when he writes, "Effective religious socialization comes about through embedded practices; that is, through specific, deliberate religious activities that are firmly intertwined with the daily habits of family routines, of eating and sleeping, of having conversations, of adorning spaces in which people live, of celebrating the holidays, and of being part of a community" (Wuthnow, xxxi–ii).

Wuthnow's list of common family activities that surfaced repeatedly in the research include: 1) eating together, especially the power of Sunday meals and holidays; 2) praying: bedtime rituals and prayer, grace before meals, family Seder; 3) having family conversations; 4) displaying sacred objects and religious images, especially the Bible; 5) celebrating holidays; 6) providing moral instruction; 7) engaging in family devotions and reading the Bible.

Wuthnow found that spiritual practices were woven into the very fiber of people's being; it was a total immersion. For these people, being religious was a way of life. "The daily round of family activities must somehow be brought into the presence of God. Parents praying, families eating together, conversations focusing on what is proper and improper, and sacred artifacts are all important ways in which family space is sacralized. They come together, forming an almost imperceptible mirage of experience" (Wuthnow, 8).

We need to provide a variety activities and resources for each of the eight faith-forming processes delivered in different formats, but especially in digital formats, that can reach families where they live and where they go. We now have the ability to connect with families anytime, anyplace, and just-in-time by using digital content delivered to their mobile devices (phones and tablets). Because of the abundance of faith-forming digital content now available we can provide mobile content for a family to use at the dinner table, in the car, in the morning or at bedtime, or for a mom or dad to use while waiting for their children participating in sports, music, and arts (more about this later).

Second, we need to focus on parents. Parent faith formation helps parents and grandparents grow in faith and discipleship and practice a vital and informed Christian faith. This can happen through parents' and grandparents' participation in intergenerational faith formation at church and participation in church life. It can also happen through targeted programs of theological and biblical formation for parents and grandparents—at church or online—in a variety of learning formats to make it easy for them to access the educational opportunities.

Parenting for faith-growth training develops parents' and grandparents' faith-forming skills, teaches them how to parent for faith growth, and demonstrates how to be a role model for children and adolescents in the Christian faith. This skill building can be woven into each of the eight faith-forming processes so that parents develop skills and access content for developing caring relationships, celebrating the season of the church year at home, celebrating rituals and milestones, learning the Christian tradition, praying, reading the Bible, serving those in need, and worshipping as a family with the faith community.

A curriculum for family faith formation includes strengthening family life by focusing on the assets that build strong families. In *The American Families Asset Study*, The Search Institute identified key qualities, assets, which help all kinds of families become strong. The study found that strong families keep youth safe, help each other learn and pursue their deep interests, create opportunities to connect with others, teach youth to make good decisions, foster positive identity and values, nurture spiritual development, build social-emotional skills, and encourage healthy life habits.

The research study discovered twenty-one "Family Assets" that contribute to building a healthy and strong family life. When families have more of these research-based assets, the children, adolescents, and adults in the family do better in life. The Family Assets are organized into five categories:

1. *Nurturing relationships:* positive communication, affection, emotional openness, encouragement for pursuing talents and interests.

2. *Establishing routines:* family meals, shared activities, meaningful traditions (holidays, rituals, celebrations), dependability.

3. *Maintaining expectations:* openness about tough topics, fair rules, defined boundaries, clear expectations, contributions to family.

4. *Adapting to challenges:* management of daily commitments, adaptability problem-solving, democratic decision-making.

5. *Connecting to the community:* neighborhood cohesion, relationship with others in the community, participating in enriching activities, supportive resources in the community (*The American Family Asset Study,* Search Institute).

These assets can be utilized as the foundation for whole-family programs, parent programs, online resources and training, mentoring for parents, and much more—all directed toward building healthy and strong family life.

A curriculum for family faith formation includes developing the knowledge, skills, and confidence of parents (and grandparents) for parenting. We know from the *Families and Faith* study that parents who demonstrate a close, warm, and affirming parenting style have higher religious transmission rates than cold, distant, or authoritarian parenting styles. In "What Makes a Good Parent?" Dr. Robert Epstein identifies the ten most effective child-rearing practices—all derived from published studies and ranked based on how well they predict a strong parent-child bond and children's happiness, health, and success.

1. *Love and affection.* Parents support and accept the child, are physically affectionate, and spend quality one-on-one time together.

2. *Stress management.* Parents take steps to reduce stress for themselves and their child, practice relaxation techniques, and promote positive interpretations of events.

3. *Relationship skills.* Parents maintain a healthy relationship with their spouse, significant other or co-parent, and model effective relationship skills with other people.

4. *Autonomy and independence.* Parents treat their child with respect and encourage him or her to become self-sufficient and self-reliant.

5. *Education and learning.* Parents promote and model learning and provide educational opportunities for their child.

6. *Life skills.* Parents provide for their child, have a steady income, and plan for the future.

7. *Behavior management.* Parents make extensive use of positive reinforcement and punish only when other methods of managing behavior have failed.

8. *Health.* Parents model a healthy lifestyle and good habits, such as regular exercise and proper nutrition for their child.

9. Religion. Parents support spiritual or religious development and participate in spiritual or religious activities.

10. *Safety.* Parents take precautions to protect their child and maintain awareness of the child's activities and friends

We can provide programs, resources, and support to help parents develop effective parenting and child-rearing practices that are conducive to building strong families and promoting faith transmission—offered in a variety of learning formats to make it easy for parents and grandparents to participate.

Intergenerational Faith Community and Family Faith Formation at Home

Missional Faith Formation

Missional faith formation focuses on the spiritual and religious needs of the "unchurched" and "de-churched," those who are spiritual but not religious or unaffiliated and uninterested in religion.

Research and descriptions of the characteristics of these two groups (see Chapter 1) are now available. Among high school youth we have seen the rise of Avoiders and Atheists (*A Faith of Their Own*). Among the young adults in their 20s and 30s we have seen the distinct profiles of the Religiously Indifferent, Religiously Disconnected, and Irreligious (*Souls in Transition*); and the Wanderers and Rejecters (*Hemorrhaging Faith*). Linda Mercadante organized the spiritual but not religious into five types (from the least to the most spiritual): Dissenters, Casuals, Explorers, Seekers, and Immigrants. This research provides the basis for developing targeted approaches and strategies for connecting with and engaging the "unchurched" and "de-churched."

Barna Research asked the unchurched to rate how much influence thirty different approaches had on their interest in attending a church. The three approaches that seemed to have the most positive effect were:

- developing relationships through an invitation from a trusted friend
- an appealing event—such as a concert or seminar—hosted at the church
- reputational appeal as reflected in ministries that serve the poor and providing mentoring and development for young people

Two additional ideas had moderate appeal:

- participating in a house church rather than conventional church ministry
- participating in a gathering of people from their same age group and general lifestyle (Barna and Kinnaman, 155–159)

Missional faith formation expands and extends the church's presence through outreach, connection, relationship building, and engagement with people where they live—moving faith formation out into the community. This involves developing targeted approaches and strategies designed around the particular needs and life situations of the unchurched and de-churched. These approaches and strategies need to be contextual—built around the congregation, community, and the needs of people. Missional faith formation can reach the spiritual but not religious and the unaffiliated and uninterested by using adaptable strategies, such as the following:

- Developing community settings for church ministries and faith formation by celebrating weekly worship in a community center, offering courses and workshops in a school or community center or coffee shop, and more.

- Opening church events and programs to the whole community such as vacation Bible school.
- Creating a vibrant and inviting website and an active Facebook page to connect with people.
- Connecting with people's life issues and situations by offering career mentoring, job referrals, parenting courses, life skills courses, and more.
- Connecting with people during transitions and milestone moments such as marriage, birth of a baby, graduations, funerals, and more.
- Developing high-quality, relationship-building events designed to draw people from the wider community into relationships with people from your church such as social events, concerts, service projects, and children's programs.
- Organizing small groups on a variety of themes from life centered to faith centered that meet in a variety of locations (homes, coffee shops, community centers), for example: life situation groups (moms, dads), interest or activity groups, discipleship groups, spiritual sharing groups, Bible study groups, theology study groups, service groups, prayer or spiritual disciplines groups, support groups, and study-action groups.
- Sponsoring community-wide service days and service projects that are open to everyone.
- Creating digital initiatives that reach everyone such as conducting parenting webinars that are offered online.

Missional faith formation provides pathways for people to consider or reconsider the Christian faith, to encounter Jesus and the good news, and to live as disciples in a supportive faith community. Congregations need to develop intentional and deliberate faith formation approaches that move people from discovery to exploration to commitment. Here are four examples that illustrate pathways for people to move from belonging to behaving to believing.

1. The *Catechumenate* of the early church, now restored for the contemporary church, provides a guided process moving from evangelization (inquiry) to catechesis (formation) to spiritual discernment (during Lent) to a ritual celebration of commitment (Baptism-Eucharist-Confirmation at the Easter Vigil) to post-baptismal faith formation (mystagogy). The formation component provides a holistic learning process: formation through participation in the life of the faith community, education in Scripture and the Christian tradition, apprenticeship in the Christian life, intimate connection with the liturgy and rituals of the church, moral formation, development of a life of prayer, and engagement in actions of justice and service. The journey from inquiry through formation to commitment

and a life of discipleship within a faith community is a process that can be applied to all types of situations and settings for people of all ages.

2. The *Alpha Course* covers the basics of Christianity, addressing questions like: Who is Jesus? and Why did he die? The Alpha course usually lasts ten weeks, with a day or weekend getaway in the middle. Each week, guests gather for about two hours. They share an informal meal, sing a few songs, listen to a talk on how Christianity approaches the question at hand, and then gather into small groups for discussion. The talks each week act as a springboard for small group discussions. Alpha is an open door to people outside the church. It's a way for those who are not believers or churchgoers to come and learn what Christianity is all about. It's informal and relaxed so people can drop their defenses and ask their questions. It's about exploration and discovery.

3. *Christian Life and Service Seminars* (C.L.A.S.S.) is offered by Saddleback Church to teach people what it looks like to follow Christ and give them tools they need for each step of the journey. Class 101 is an introduction to Saddleback Church, what the church believes, and how to become a member of the Saddleback family. In Class 201 people find out what it means to be more like Jesus, learn how to spend time with God through prayer and Bible study, discover the importance of tithing, and understand the value of community. In Class 301 people learn how God can use their spiritual gifts, heart (passions), abilities, personality, and experiences to help to others. Class 401 helps people discover their calling, learn how to share their story with others, write down their personal testimony, and see how to impact the world with Christ's love.

4. *Lifetree Café* offers people the opportunity to gather in warm and hospitable venues to explore life and faith. Simply put, it's a "conversation café"—a place and time for people to gather weekly to experience stories and talk about thought-provoking topics relating to life and faith. The hour-long Lifetree Café experiences feature stories of real people, guided conversation, biblical insights, time to build relationships with new and old friends, laughter, fun, and opportunities to serve. Lifetree brings people together to explore important and intriguing life issues, serve the community, and experience God through Jesus Christ.

Online and Digitally Enabled Faith Formation

The digital revolution has transformed almost every aspect of society. No facet of this revolution has more potential than its ability to change the way people learn. The availability of a vast array of knowledge and resources at the click of a mouse or the touch of a screen, together with the ability to connect instantaneously with peers and mentors across the street and around the world, make possible completely new learning environments and experiences. These opportunities are highly engaging and collaborative, and they are based on learners' own interests and strengths. People can truly learn anytime, anyplace, and at any pace today.

We have never had access to better technologies and resources for nurturing growth in Christian faith with all ages and equipping people to live as disciples of Jesus Christ in the world today. The new technologies and resources of the digital era provide tremendous opportunities for congregational faith formation to thrive in the twenty-first century. Just as an earlier era adopted the new technologies of the day—schooling and the printing press—to produce educational models using classrooms and teachers, catechisms and textbooks, the twenty-first century has digital technologies, tools, and media that can be utilized to create new models that will transform faith formation in a congregation.

We need to embrace **the abundance of new digital technologies and media for learning and faith formation** that is unprecedented in history—the Internet, Wi-Fi and broadband connectivity, interactive web platforms, mobile devices (phones, tablets, laptops), digital video websites (YouTube and more), social media (Facebook, Twitter, Instagram, and more), online conferencing (Skype, Google+ Hangouts, and more), and digital tools for creating online classrooms, videos, games, etc.

We need to utilize **the abundance of high-quality digital religious content and experiences** found in websites, blogs, apps, e-books, video, and much more—created by individuals, publishers, congregations, religious organizations—and often free.

We need to create **new models of faith formation that utilize the digital technologies and digital media** to engage people with faith-forming content anytime, any place, just-in-time; and that can extend and expand faith formation in physical, face-to-face settings into people's daily lives through digital content and mobile delivery systems. We can develop blended models of faith formation that incorporate physical settings and online settings. These settings can be seen as a continuum: ranging from fully online programming to gathered programming in physical settings that use online resources. Blended faith formation usually combines online delivery of religious content and experiences with the best features of gathered face-to-face programs. Here is a view of the five models on a continuum (more about this in Chapter 3).

Blended Faith Formation Continuum

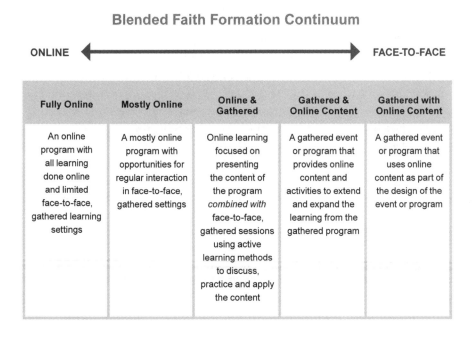

ONLINE ⬅————————————————————➡ FACE-TO-FACE

Fully Online	Mostly Online	Online & Gathered	Gathered & Online Content	Gathered with Online Content
An online program with all learning done online and limited face-to-face, gathered learning settings	A mostly online program with opportunities for regular interaction in face-to-face, gathered settings	Online learning focused on presenting the content of the program *combined with* face-to-face, gathered sessions using active learning methods to discuss, practice and apply the content	A gathered event or program that provides online content and activities to extend and expand the learning from the gathered program	A gathered event or program that uses online content as part of the design of the event or program

CONCLUSION

There is no going back to the old faith formation ecosystem. We now have "to boldly go where no one (in congregational faith formation) has gone before."

We *can* provide lifelong faith formation for all ages and generations across a ten-decade life cycle. We *can* address the changing patterns of America society (ethnic cultures, generations, families). We *can* respond to the diverse religious beliefs and practices of people today. We *can* create new ways to promote religious transmission from generation to generation.

The new faith formation ecosystem provides us with an approach that addresses these challenges through its five interconnected components:

- intergenerational faith formation in the congregation
- age-group and generational faith formation in a variety of physical places and online spaces
- family faith formation at home
- missional faith formation to the spiritual but not religious and the unaffiliated
- online and digitally enabled faith formation

Each component makes an important contribution to a comprehensive approach to faith formation with all ages and generations. To review the faith-forming ecosystem in your congregation, use the "Reimagining Faith Formation" Assessment Tool (on page 134) with church staff and faith formation leaders. (It also is available online at www.21stCenturyFaithFormation.com.)

The New Faith Formation Ecosystem

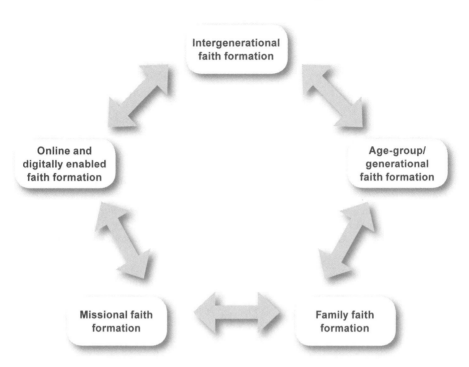

A new model of faith formation and learning can bring to life interconnected components of the new faith formation ecosystem in a practical way for congregations. Chapter 3 introduces a network model of faith formation that seeks to do just this.

Works Cited

Allen, Holly and Christine Ross. *Intergenerational Christian Formation*. Downers Grove, IL: IVP Academic, 2012.

Alpha USA. The Alpha Course (http://guest.alphausa.org; and http://www.alphausa.org/Groups/1000060778/For_my_Church.aspx)

Barna, George, and David Kinnaman. *Churchless*. Carol Stream, IL: Tyndale Momentum, 2014. (also https://www.barna.org/churchless#.VMdqTcZLzds)

Bass, Diana Butler. *Christianity after Religion*. San Francisco: HarperOne, 2012.

Bengston, Vern with Norella M. Putney and Susan Harris. *Families and Faith: How Religion Is Passed Down across Generations*. New York: Oxford University Press, 2013.

Bunge, Marcia. "Biblical and Theological Perspectives and Best Practices for Faith Formation." *Understanding Children's Spirituality*. Edited by Kevin Lawson. Eugene, OR: Cascade Books, 2012.

The Charter for Lifelong Christian Formation. The Episcopal Church, July 2009. (www.episcopalchurch.org/sites/default/files/downloads/formationcharter_8.5x11_f.pdf.)

Dollahite, David, and Loren Marks. "How Highly Religious Families Strive to Fulfill Sacred Purposes." *Sourcebook on Family Theories and Methods*. Edited by Bengston, V., D. Klein, A. Acock, K. Allen, and P. Dilworth-Anderson. Thousand Oaks, CA: Sage Publications, 2005.

Epstein, Robert. "What Makes a Good Parent?: A Scientific Analysis Ranks the 10 Most Effective Child-Rearing Practices." *Scientific American Mind*, November/December 2010, (pages 46–51).

Foster, Charles. *From Generation to Generation: The Adaptive Challenge of Mainline Protestant Education in Forming Faith*. Eugene, OR: Cascade Books, 2012.

Fuller, Buckminster. "Quotes." (http://www.goodreads.com/author/quotes/165737.Buckminster_Fuller)

Groome, Thomas. *Will There Be Faith: A New Vision for Educating and Growing Disciples*. New York: HarperOne, 2011.

Harris, Maria. *Fashion Me A People*. Louisville: Westminster/John Knox, 1988.

Lifetree Café. (www.lifetreecafe.com.)

Martinson, Roland, Wes Black, and John Roberto. *The Spirit and Culture of Youth Ministry*. St. Paul: EYM Publications, 2010.

Mercadante, Linda. *Belief with Borders: Inside the Minds of the Spiritual but not Religious*. New York: Oxford University Press, 2014.

Mercer, Joyce Ann. "Cultivating a Community Practice." Patheos.com, August 13, 2013. (www.patheos.com/Topics/Passing-on-the-Faith/Community-Practice-Joyce-Ann-Mercer-08-14-2013.html.)

Pearce, Lisa D., and Melinda Lundquist Denton. *A Faith of Their Own*. New York: Oxford University Press, 2011.

Pink, Daniel. Drive: *The Surprising Truth About What Motivates Us*. New York: Riverhead, 2009.

"Re-imaging Learning in the 21st Century." MacArthur Foundation, Digital Media and Learning Network, 2010.

Saddleback Church. Class 101–401. (http://saddleback.com/connect/ministry/class)

Smith, Christian with Patricia Snell. *Souls in Transition: The Religious and Spiritual Lives of Emerging Adults*. New York: Oxford University Press, 2009.

Syvertsen, Amy, K., Eugene C. Roehlkepartain, and Peter C. Scales. *The American Family Assets Study*. Minneapolis: Search Institute, 2012. (http://www.search-institute.org/research/family-strengths)

Westerhoff, John. *Will Our Children Have Faith?* New York: Morehouse, 2012.

Wuthnow, Robert. *Growing Up Religious*. Boston: Beacon Press, 1999.

CHAPTER 3

REIMAGINING THE MODEL

You never change things by fighting the existing reality.
To change something, build a new model that makes the existing model obsolete.
(Buckminster Fuller)

We are witnessing transformations in the way we think about learning, reflecting the convergence of new technologies, digital media and tools, and network thinking. The MacArthur Foundation's Digital Media and Learning Project identified three major transformations:

A shift from education to learning. Education is what institutions do—learning is what people do. Digital media enable learning anywhere, anytime; formal learning must be mobile and just-in-time.

A shift from consumption of information to participatory learning. A new system of learning must be peer based and organized around learners' interests, enabling them to create as well as consume information. It encourages learners to experiment and create, to produce and design things.

A shift from institutions to networks. In the digital age, the fundamental operating and delivery systems are networks, not institutions such as schools, which are a node on a person's network of learning opportunities. People learn across institutions, so an entire learning network must be supported ("Re-imagining Learning in the 21st Century").

A revolution in technology has transformed the way we find each other, interact, and collaborate to create knowledge as connected learners. What are connected learners? Learners who collaborate online; learners who use social media to connect with others around the globe; learners who engage in conversations in online spaces; and learners who bring what they learn back to inform their schools, workplaces, communities, and the world.

The "Connected Learning" approach developed by a team at the Digital Media and Learning Research Hub and supported by the MacArthur Foundation provides insights into the transformation of learning in the digital age. Connected Learning is anchored in research, robust theories of learning, and the best of traditional standards, but also designed to mine the learning potential of the new social and digital media domain. It harnesses the advances and innovations of our connected age to serve learning. Just as earlier generations tapped the tools of their time to improve learning, we must do the same in the digital age.

The Connected Learning approach can be summarized in the following characteristics:

Interests. Interests foster the drive to gain knowledge and expertise. Research has repeatedly shown that when the topic is personally interesting and relevant, learners achieve much higher-order learning outcomes. Connected learning views interests and passions that are developed in a social context as essential elements.

Peer Culture. Connected learning thrives in a socially meaningful and knowledge-rich ecology of ongoing participation, self-expression, and recognition. In their everyday exchanges with peers and friends, young people fluidly contribute, share, and give feedback. Powered with possibilities made available by today's social media, this peer culture can produce learning that's engaging and powerful.

Production-centered. Connected learning prizes the learning that comes from actively producing, creating, experimenting, and designing because it promotes skills and dispositions for lifelong learning, and for making meaningful contributions to today's world.

Shared purpose. Today's social media and web-based communities provide unprecedented opportunities for children, youth, adults, parents, and teachers to share interests and contribute to a common purpose. The potential for cross-generational learning and connection unfolds when centered on common goals.

Openly networked. Connected learning environments link learning in school, home, and community because learners achieve best when their learning is reinforced and supported in multiple settings. Online platforms can make learning resources abundant, accessible, and visible across all learning settings (Ito, et al.).

Connected Learning is active, relevant, real world, effective, hands-on, networked, innovative, personal, and transformative. It connects three critical spheres of learning: academics, a learner's interests, inspiring mentors and peers. (See the appendix Connected Learning Principles on page 81.)

Another important trend is the personalizing of learning, facilitated by learning networks, digital content, social connectivity, and devices to connect with the content and people. Katherine Prince has outlined the features of a "Vibrant Learning Grid" in which educational leaders can create a flexible and personalized learning ecosystem that meets the needs of all learners. She describes several of its key features:

- Learners will move seamlessly across many kinds of learning experiences and providers, with teachers and learning guides supporting them in customizing and carrying out their learning journeys.
- The ways in which we organize learning will diversify, with "school" taking more forms.
- Learning will no longer be defined by time and place—unless a learner wants to learn at a particular time and in a particular place.
- Learners (and their families) will create individualized learning playlists reflecting their particular interests, goals, and values. Those playlists might include schools but also a wide variety of digitally mediated or place-based learning experiences—at museums, science centers, libraries, and more (Price 16–17).

At the heart of this transition to twenty-first century learning is the question: What if learning adapted to each person instead of expecting each person to adapt to the school or the curriculum or the program?

The central themes of the transformation in learning need to be central features of congregational faith formation: putting learners at the center of our thinking; enabling and trusting learners to be co-creators of their learning experiences; connecting learning authentically to life concerns and real world issues; making room for new modes of learning and new methods of teaching; fostering collaboration in learning; and organizing structures around learners' needs.

Congregations can embrace the transformations happening in the world of learning. We will need a new model that embodies the best developments in learning and brings to life the interconnected components of the new faith formation ecosystem in a practical way.

A NEW MODEL:
THE FAITH FORMATION NETWORK

In an earlier era if you wanted to learn more about the Bible, you could take a Bible course at a fixed time—at a church, seminary, college, or other education provider, or read a book—perhaps recommended by your pastor and borrowed from your church's library, or watch a video—on VHS of course! Your options would have been limited. In the twenty-first century if you want to learn more about the Bible, your options are greatly expanded. You could do any combination of the following:

1. Take a course at church or college or seminary.

2. Take a course online—at a scheduled time with a group or at your own time and pace.

3. Read and view videos online at a Bible website, such as www.entertheBible. org from Luther Seminary.

4. Join an online Bible study group at another church or on Facebook.

5. Watch a video series on YouTube from a scripture scholar, such as N.T. Wright, as you read his book or watch a video series produced by another congregation that is available for free on their website.

6. Find a mentor in your community or online who will guide your self-directed Bible study.

7. Listen to audio versions of your book(s) using your smartphone as you commute to work each day.

8. Download a Bible study app, engage in daily Bible readings and reflections, and share your reflections with others who are studying the Bible using the app and social media.

9. Create a blog to post your thoughts on what you are learning and invite others to offer their insights.

10. Organize your own learning group by gathering a group of people who are interested in learning more about the Bible and using print, audio, video, and online resources to guide your small group.

In this example we see the shift to a networked approach to learning for an individual. Learners now have the ability to construct their own networks of learning, utilizing a variety of new technologies and the abundance of high-quality print, audio, video, and online resources that are readily available to them. Learning networks not only provide access to a virtually endless array of learning opportunities, but can offer learners multiple points of entry that provide individualized pathways of learning and faith growth.

What if we reimagined congregational faith formation as a network of relationships, content, experiences, and resources—in physical places and online spaces? This networked model of faith formation is *lifelong*—each stage of life from birth to death—and *life-wide*—everywhere, anytime learning within a network of mentors, teachers, family, and peers. It provides a wide variety of engaging and interactive content and experiences in online and physical settings (home, congregation, community, world). It offers faith formation content and experiences to respond to the diverse religious and spiritual needs of people today—from the spiritually committed and engaged to the spiritual but not religious and the unaffiliated. It enables congregations to become centers for lifelong learning and faith growth for *all* people by utilizing the best of the new digital technologies to bring an abundance of meaningful and engaging faith-forming experiences—in the congregation and the world, and in a variety of media—to people of all ages.

Adopting a network approach to congregation faith formation reflects the fact that we are living in the age of networks.

> Networks are everywhere. The brain is a network of nerve cells connected by axons, and cells themselves are networks of molecules connected by biochemical reactions. Societies, too, are networks of people linked by friendships, familial relationships and professional ties. On a larger scale, food webs and ecosystems can be represented as networks of species. And networks pervade technology: the Internet, power grids and transportation systems are but a few examples. Even the language we are using to convey these thoughts to you is a network, made up of words connected by syntactic relationships (Barabasi and Bonabeau, 52).

Images of networks appear in the Scriptures. Jesus uses the image of the vine and branches to describe his relationship with the disciples (church) and their relationship with him: "I am the true vine, and my Father is the vinegrower. . . . Abide in me as I abide in you. Just as the branch cannot bear fruit by itself unless it abides in the vine, neither can you unless you abide in me. I am the vine, you are the branches. Those who abide in me and I in them bear much fruit, because apart from me you can do nothing" (John 15:1, 4–5).

Paul uses the image of the body to describe the early Christian community. "For just as the body is one and has many members, and all the members of the body, though many, are one body, so it is with Christ. For in the one Spirit we were all baptized into one body—Jews or Greeks, slaves or free—and we were all made to drink of one Spirit" (1 Cor. 12:12–13).

We are all part of networks—our families, our schools, our workplaces, our religious congregations, our social circles, our online life. Networks—collections of people (and their resources) connected to each other through relationships—aren't new. They're as old as human society.

What is new is that in the twenty-first century this understanding of networks has been expanded to include the digital network of the Internet, the World Wide Web, and the new social media platforms and tools. New tools and technologies are changing the way we communicate and connect. The changes can be seen in the way people are working together to create and disseminate knowledge. The shift is not just in the new Web 2.0 technologies. It's in the way that increasingly widespread access to these tools is driving a fundamental change in how groups are formed and work gets done. Today we can turn to people, organizations, and resources anywhere in the world to help us answer questions, connect to relevant content and resources, or just share our life experiences and stories. These new approaches to connecting people and organizing work are now allowing us to do old things in new ways and to try completely new things that weren't possible before.

Another way to view the network vision of life and church is Keith Anderson's image of the *digital cathedral*, which evokes "an expansive understanding of church in a digitally-integrated world, one that extends ministry into digital and local gathering spaces, recognizes the holy in our everyday lives, and embodies a networked, relational, and incarnational ministry leadership for a digital age."

> In fact, the cathedral was not just a monumental building, as we often think of it today, but rather a networked, relational, incarnational community that included people with a surprising range of beliefs and practices. Within premodern cathedral grounds were breweries and bakeries, granaries and gardens, monasteries and markets. Beyond the walls, the cathedral proper extended to the forests, fields, and villages where a diverse array of ordinary believers found the sacred in their waking and their sleeping, their toils and their leisure. People lived life fully "in cathedral"—in relationship to one another within an expansive, everyday understanding of "church."
>
> Well, today, the places that are "in cathedral" are both local and digital—coffee shops, pubs, and parks; Facebook, Twitter, and Instagram—as well as in the digitally-integrated connections people with smartphones and tablets make between their local participation and their digital networks.
>
> What if we were to reclaim this larger sense of "cathedral" and "church"—one that encompasses our daily working and living, that includes both local spaces like pubs, coffee shops, and parks, but also digital gathering spaces such as Facebook, Twitter, Instagram, and YouTube? How can we understand all of these online and offline spaces as part of an expansive, networked whole? And how would this shift our practice of ministry, our leadership, and our assumptions about the loci of spiritual practice?
>
> In this view, the spiritual life experienced "in cathedral" would include not just worship at the local church building, but also a family bustling through breakfast on the way to school and work. It would extend to bus stops, classrooms, coffee shops, offices, cafés, and so on, all of these holding the potential of further connection through smartphones, tablets, and

laptops. In this digital cathedral, any node in the network can mediate the divine in everyday life, can function as sacred space. Here, our lowly digital devices invite pilgrimage every day across these networked sacred spaces.

Imagined this way, the digital cathedral is not a call to return to a time when church was at the center of the culture—even if that were possible. Rather, it is a warm, digitally-integrated embrace of the rich traditions of Christianity, especially the recovery of the premodern sense of cathedral, which encompassed the depth and breadth of daily life within the physical and imaginative landscape of the church.

Anderson's understanding of the digital cathedral is a great way to imagine a networked approach to life, learning, and church. (See his book *The Digital Cathedral: Networked Ministry in a Wireless World*.)

Twenty-first century faith formation will look and feel and operate as a network. It will no longer resemble the linear, one size fits all model of the industrial age. As a network it will provide a diversity of religious content and experiences for all ages and generations, 24x7x365, in face-to-face (physical) and online (virtual) settings. It will incorporate an immense range of faith formation opportunities.

CHARACTERISTICS OF FAITH FORMATION IN A NETWORK MODEL

Variety of Content, Method, Format, and Delivery

In a network model, faith formation is designed around the life tasks, needs, interests, and spiritual journeys of individuals and families across the whole life span.

We are moving from a provider-centered, program-driven model where denominations, publishers, and churches determined the curriculum to a *learner-centered model* where the content and experiences are designed around the people and where they have control over their learning. Individuals and families have an active role in shaping their own learning and moving along personal trajectories of faith growth. A faith formation network provides a congregation with a means to offer relevant content that addresses the spiritual and religious needs of people *and* the ability for them to engage with that content in ways that reflect how they learn and grow best. A network approach provides more options for people of all ages to find programs, activities, and resources that match well with how they learn and grow in faith.

Faith formation provides a variety of learning experiences that can engage the whole person in learning. Faith formation networks address the whole person and how they learn best by offering programs, activities, and resources that emphasize different "intelligences"—word-centered, verbal–linguistic, logical, musical, visual, intrapersonal, interpersonal, naturalist, and bodily-kinesthetic (see the work of Howard Gardner). While it may be difficult to incorporate all eight intelligences in a particular program or activity, a network approach provides a way to offer programs, activities, and resources that emphasize different "intelligences"—one that is word-centered, another musical, another visual, etc.—so as to engage as many people as possible.

People have different learning styles. Some learn best through direct, hands-on, concrete experiences; some through reflective observation; some through an exploration and analysis of knowledge, theories, and concepts; and others through active experimentation with the new knowledge and practices. A network provides a way to offer programs reflecting the four different learning styles, such as immersion programs, workshops, presentations, small group study, and retreat experiences to name a few.

Faith formation provides a variety of experiences, programs, activities, resources, and social connections that are available anytime and anywhere, in physical places and online spaces, and conducted in variety of settings— self-directed, mentored, at home, in small groups, in large groups, church-wide, in the community, and in the world. We are moving from the one size fits all curriculum and programming of an earlier era to a variety of religious content— experiences, programs, activities, and resources—that connects with people's spiritual and religious needs. A network approach gives us the ability to offer activities that target the particular spiritual or religious needs, interests, passions, concerns, or life issues of individuals, families, and groups. We no longer have to worry about reaching a mass audience with one size fits all programming. We can diversify faith formation offerings and tailor them to people's needs and busy lives.

This movement from one sizes fits all to a variety of faith formation offerings is made possible by the abundance of religious content—print, audio, video, online, and digital—and programming that is now available. And this is made possible by the creation of an online platform that integrates, delivers, and communicates the content and programming with a variety of ways to learn and that is easily accessible and available, anytime and anywhere. In the network model faith formation becomes personal, portable, and participatory—the key characteristics of the mobile technology revolution.

A faith formation network incorporates seven learning environments, in online spaces and physical places, to provide a variety of ways for people to learn and grow in faith that respects their preferred styles of learning, their life situations, and their time constraints. The seven environments provide a way to offer the same content or program in multiple learning environments, giving people different ways to learn and grow in faith. The seven environments include:

- on your own (self-directed)
- with a mentor
- at home
- in small groups
- in large groups
- in the congregation
- in the community and world

A variety of learning methods can be used with each of these seven learning environments. Creating this variety of learning environments is aided by the development of an online platform that integrates, delivers, and communicates the faith formation offerings.

Faith formation incorporates formal and informal learning. Informal learning describes a lifelong process whereby individuals acquire attitudes, values, skills, and knowledge from daily experience and the educational influences and resources in their environment, from family and neighbors, from work and play, from the marketplace, the library, the mass media, and the Internet. Informal learning can be intentional or not. There might be a teacher, but it's probably a colleague or friend. We might read an article or book, visit a website, listen to a podcast, or watch a video online. We might visit Home Depot or Lowe's for a clinic on home repair or gardening or stop by our local bookstore or library for a reading group or special program. We might go online to access any one of the thousands of "how to" videos on YouTube. We might watch one of the TV channels devoted to informal learning, such as cooking channels that teach people how to cook and try new recipes or home improvement shows that present examples and teach techniques.

Both formal and informal learning can be *intentional*—when an individual aims to learn something and goes about achieving that objective or *unexpected*—when in the course of everyday activities an individual learns something that he or she had not intended or expected. Most faith formation programs are formal and intentional learning. We can expand *informal* and *intentional* faith formation when we make available a variety online activities, print resources, audio podcasts, videos, apps, and more that people can access on their own, anytime, anywhere.

Personalized Learning and Faith Growth

Faith formation provides the opportunity for personalized and customized learning and faith growth, giving people an active role in shaping their own learning and moving along their own personal trajectories of faith growth. People are guided by trusted guides who find the right programs, activities, and resources to match with their learning needs.

We know from learning sciences research that more effective learning will occur if each person receives a customized learning experience. People learn best when they are placed in a learning environment that is sensitive to their learning needs and flexible enough to adapt strategies and resources to individual needs. We can now meet people at the point of their spiritual, religious, and learning needs and offer personalized pathways for faith growth.

A faith formation network, rich in a diversity of content and a variety of ways to learn, can guide people in creating their own personal learning pathways. Churches can develop processes for helping individuals and families diagnose their religious and spiritual learning needs (online and in person) that:

- discern learning needs
- create a plan (with a mentor/guide) for faith growth and find resources on the network
- engage in faith formation experiences
- reflect on [their] learning with a mentor/guide or small group
- identify new needs for growth and learning

A "faith-growth learning plan" helps people identify where they are on their spiritual journey, what they need for continuing their growth, who else might share that need, and the resources that could help them meet that need. Giving power to individuals and families to shape their own learning does not mean abandoning them to their own devices. Congregations provide mentors or guides to assist people in developing their growth plan, accessing the programs and resources that fit their plan, and evaluating their learning.

The Flow of Personalized Learning

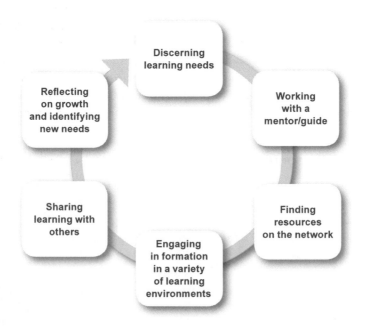

Imagine redesigning confirmation by moving from a one-size-fits-all approach to a personalized approach using a network. Imagine beginning with discernment so that young people, with the help of a mentor, can talk about their faith journey; then determining the content and activities from the "confirmation network" that are most appropriate to their religious and spiritual needs; participating in those activities—on their own, with a mentor, at home, in small groups, in large groups, in the congregation, and/or in the community and world; and then reflecting with their mentor on their growth.

A Process of Active Inquiry and Intrinsic Motivation

Faith formation recognizes that learning is a process of active inquiry with the initiative residing within the individual. Faith formation networks recognize that the motivation for learning is intrinsic to the person and is driven by a need for autonomy (self-directedness), mastery, and purpose and meaning.

The traditional model of schooling has conditioned people to perceive the proper role of learners as being dependent on teachers to make decisions for them as to what should be learned, how it should be learned, when it should be learned, and if it has been learned. Today people are accustomed to searching out what they want to know, when they want and need to know it. People are becoming more and more self-directed in their learning, and they have almost unlimited access to information through the Internet and the wide variety of print and media learning resources available in our society today.

As learning becomes a process of active inquiry, where the initiative resides within the person, intrinsic motivation becomes a key factor in determining whether or not people will engage in faith formation and open themselves to learning and faith growth. Extrinsic motivation, such as faith formation participation polices (such as required hours or things that must be done in order to receive a sacrament), rarely motivate people to participate, learn, or grow in faith. In fact, they usually have the opposite effect.

Drawing on decades of scientific research on human motivation, Daniel Pink in his book *Drive: The Surprising Truth about What Motivates Us* exposes the mismatch between what research shows and how we motivate people. While carrots and sticks (policies and requirements) worked somewhat successfully in the twentieth-century, assembly-line model, that's precisely the wrong way to motivate people today. He describes three types of motivation: Motivation 1.0 presumed that humans were biological creatures, struggling for survival. Motivation 2.0 presumed that humans responded to reward and punishments in their environment. Motivation 3.0 presumes that humans have a third drive—to learn, to create, and to better the world. Motivation 3.0 has three essential elements.

Autonomy: the desire to direct our own lives with autonomy over task (what they do), time (when they do it), team (who they do it with), and technique (how they do it).

Mastery: the urge to get better and better at something that matters—to be engaged in deliberate practice to produce mastery.

Purpose: the yearning to do what we do in the service of something larger than ourselves, to seek purpose—a cause greater and more enduring than ourselves.

Daniel Pink writes, "The secret to high performance and satisfaction—at work, at school, and at home—is the deeply human need to direct our own lives, to learn and create new things, and to do better by ourselves and our world (145)." Learning and growth in a faith formation network is a process of active inquiry, where the initiative resides within the person. Intrinsic motivation—autonomy, mastery, purpose and meaning— become key factors in determining whether or not people will engage in faith formation and open themselves to learning and faith growth.

Here is one example of how autonomy and mastery combine to motivate learners. A recent research study found that students want control of their own learning. When asked why learning through an online class might make school more interesting, 47 percent of students in grades 9–12, 39 percent in grades 6–8, and 25 percent in grades 3–5 responded that they wanted to learn online to control their own learning experience. Students do not expect online courses to be easier. They do, however, expect the online learning environment to facilitate their success because they can review materials when they want and are more comfortable asking teachers for help. And online teachers see great benefits to student online learning: 76 percent believe that online learning benefits students by putting them in control of their own learning.

Communities of Faith Learning and Practice

Faith formation intentionally nurtures communities of learning and practice around the shared interests, needs, life stages, and activities of individuals and families.

Faith formation can connect individuals and families to each other through communities of practice—groups of people who have a shared interest, passion, religious or spiritual need, life stage—who come together to learn with and from each other. William Synder describes communities of practice having three dimensions: "the domain (what it's about); the topic (the issues that they are facing); and the community (the people who are involved)."

In a network approach, groups form naturally as individuals and families connect with others around shared interests, passions, needs, or life stage. Participation in these groups and their shared activities develop relationships, provide a supportive community, and promote learning and the application of that learning. By creating a network with a great variety of activities, congregations can intentionally promote the natural development of communities of learning and practice around these shared activities. This is a different approach from the congregations who adopt a small group model of church and then organize people into small groups.

Oftentimes this approach can feel artificial and contrived. In a network approach groups are self-organizing around activities that reflect their interests, passions, hungers, or needs.

Imagine a group forming around a Bible study offering on the faith formation network. They may do this in a small group, but they are engaged in a larger community of practice in their congregation or in the world focused on reading and studying the Bible. People in the small group connect, face-to-face and/or online, to study the Bible together and to learn how to apply the Bible in their daily lives. They can connect with other groups, via social media, to share their experience of learning and practice. They can share their learning with the whole congregation, providing an opportunity for everyone to grow in their understanding of the Bible.

Digital Platforms for Faith Formation

Faith formation incorporates digital platforms (websites) that integrate all of the content (programs, activities, resources), connects people to the content and to each other, provides continuity for people across different learning experiences, and is available anytime, anywhere.

We can already see (and have probably personally experienced) the power of digital platforms for learning. Universities across the country are making their courses available online for free. The Khan Academy (www.khanacademy.org) is providing thousands of instructional videos for elementary and high school education for free so that students can learn on their own and teachers can "flip the classroom" by having students watch the videos (the content) as homework and transform the classroom into a laboratory for applying the content. TED.com is making available the videos of all their world-class presenters for free and TedEd (http://ed.ted.com) is becoming a platform for creating customized lessons around TED Talks.

Art museums, children's museums, natural history museums, libraries, science centers, and more are building interactive, multimedia online digital platforms for their content that serves as a second place for learning to complement their physical place. As just one example, the Boston Science Center (www.mos.org), a marvelous hands-on environment for experiencing and learning science, has built a digital platform for an online experience of the science center with their YouTube channel for their videos, a Facebook page, Pinterest boards for exhibits, Flickr photostream and Instagram sites for photos, and more. The Boston Science Center is now accessible 24x7x365 to everyone and is networked via social media.

In the digital age, congregations need to develop online digital platforms as a second place for faith formation with unique features and content, which also extends and expands programs and activities in physical settings. Increasingly churches will need to see themselves not as exclusive providers of faith formation, but as platforms for bringing meaningful and engaging learning experiences to people and for guiding them to such experiences elsewhere.

A faith formation website provides the platform for publishing and delivering the experiences, content, programs, activities, and resources of the network, and for engaging people in learning and faith formation. A website provides the platform for *seamless* learning across a variety of experiences, resources, locations, times, or settings. The website, together with social media, provides continuity between faith formation in the congregation, at home, in daily life, and online.

The technological and skill barriers for building a digital platform continue to decrease with the availability of drag and drop website builders like Weebly (www. Weebly.com), Wix (www.Wix.com), and Squarespace (www.squarespace.com). For more advanced website building there is WordPress (www.wordpress.com) with its thousands of templates and plug-ins.

Blended Faith Formation

Faith formation integrates online and face-to-face learning, blending them in a variety of ways from online programs with minimal interaction in physical settings to programs in physical settings that utilize online content or extend the program using online content.

Michael Horn and Heather Staker describe blended learning as "a formal education program in which a person learns at least in part through online learning with some element of learner control over time, place, path, and/or pace; *and* at least in part at a supervised brick-and-mortar location away from home. The modalities along each person's learning path in a course or subject are connected to provide an integrated experience" (Staker and Horn, 54).

The team at "More than Blended Learning" (http://morethanblended.com) describes a blended solution as "a learning intervention that combines a number of contrasting methods and/or media." In the methods category, we can blend by *social context*—alone, one-to-one, in a group, in a community and by *learning strategy*—exposition, instruction, guided discovery, exploration. In the media category, we can blend by *delivery channel*—face-to-face, offline media, online media, and by *communications mode*—synchronous (same-time) and asynchronous (own-time).

Faith formation programs, activities, and experiences can be offered in a variety of places, integrating physical and online settings. These settings can be seen as a continuum: ranging from fully online programming to gathered programming in physical settings that use online resources. Blended faith formation usually combines online delivery of religious content and experiences with the best features of gathered face-to-face programs.

Blended Faith Formation Continuum

ONLINE ⟵⟶ FACE-TO-FACE

Fully Online	Mostly Online	Online & Gathered	Gathered & Online Content	Gathered with Online Content
An online program with all learning done online and limited face-to-face, gathered learning settings	A mostly online program with opportunities for regular interaction in face-to-face, gathered settings	Online learning focused on presenting the content of the program *combined with* face-to-face, gathered sessions using active learning methods to discuss, practice and apply the content	A gathered event or program that provides online content and activities to extend and expand the learning from the gathered program	A gathered event or program that uses online content as part of the design of the event or program

Imagine the possibilities for utilizing the five blended strategies in designing new programming, redesigning existing programming, surrounding events and programs with online content, and selecting a variety of digital programs, activities, and resources that can be used alone (fully online) or used in conjunction with face-to-face programs.

Gathered with Online Content

We can design a gathered program using online content from websites, videos from YouTube or other video sites, and blogs and other social media. With an abundance of high-quality digital content, this first option is the easiest way to bring the digital world into a gathered program.

Gathered and Online Content

We can connect church programs or events with online content that extends and deepens the experience through learning, prayer, ritual, action, etc. Gathered events and programs, such as Sunday worship, church year feasts and seasons, intergenerational and family programs, classes, youth group meetings, mission trips, retreat experiences, and vacation Bible school would all benefit from extending the experience with digital content for learning, praying, celebrating, having faith conversations, acting/serving, and more. The eight faith-forming processes (see page 38) can serve as an organizing template for developing and selecting activities. Here are some examples:

- Extend Sunday worship through the week using a variety of digital content that deepens the understanding and practice of the Sunday readings, sermon, and church year season; and provides prayer, devotions, rituals, a video of the sermon with a study guide, service/action ideas, conversation activities, and more.
- Connect Vacation Bible School with families at home by providing activities online that deepen the content from each day of Vacation Bible School: study activities around the theme or Scripture story/message of the day, a prayer or devotion, a book to read, a video to watch, and more.
- Provide a forty-day Lent "curriculum" that connects the Lent events in church life with a variety of activities for experiencing and practicing Lent in daily and home life—delivered online through the congregation's faith formation website. Here's an illustration:

CHURCH LIFE EVENTS	DAILY AND HOME LIFE ACTIVITIES
Ash Wednesday	Fasting activities
Lent Sunday liturgies	Praying activities
Stations of the Cross	Service/almsgiving activities
Lent prayer	Lectionary reflections
Lent retreat	Lent study resources and videos
Lent service	Lent devotions
Lent soup suppers	Daily Bible readings

Online and Gathered

We can "flip the classroom or program" by creating a digital platform to provide the content that people would learn in the gathered setting in an online learning space using print, audio, video, and more. And then transform the gathered program using interactive activities, discussion, project-based learning, and practice and demonstration. Here are some examples:

- Redesign children's faith formation so that children (and their parents) are learning the content at home with online content (and/or a textbook) and doing activities with their parents at home, and then refocus "class time" to engage children in creating projects and activities that demonstrate their learning.
- Design a high school confirmation program that provides the content usually taught in the weekly sessions into an online platform for individual learning—watching videos, reading short materials, and writing a reflection

journal; engage the young people in small groups during the month to discuss their online learning; and then meet monthly in a large group gathered session for discussion, interactive activities, and application of the content to living as a Christian today. During the year, retreats, worship, and service projects offer additional gathered sessions.

- Develop an online center for justice and service where people of all ages can find a justice issue that they are passionate about, learn more about the issue, and explore biblical and Christian teaching on justice. Congregations can provide a variety of ways for people to act on their justice issue—as individuals, families, or groups, through local and global projects. People can share their experiences with the whole congregation using social media.

Mostly Online

We can offer opportunities for individuals, families, and small groups to utilize the digital platform as their primary learning setting and provide opportunities for regular interaction in face-to-face, gathered settings or in a web conference format, such as a Google+ Hangout. Here are some examples:

- Offer one-hour parent webinar programs delivered to parents at home in a four-month timeframe: three monthly webinars followed by a parent gathering at church in month four.
- Offer online learning plans and resources for self-study or small group study with video recordings of adult faith formation presentations at church. Invite people to gather at the conclusion of their learning to share their insights with others who participated.
- Develop an online Bible study where groups can meet regularly in a physical setting or virtually through Skype or a Google+ Hangout for sharing their learning.
- Offer selected online courses and activities from colleges, seminaries, and religious organization through the faith formation website for individualized learning with the option for a mentor or small group gathering.

Fully Online

The rise of high-quality and easily accessible online religious content—courses, activities, print and e-books, audio and video programs, and content-rich websites—has made designing online faith formation feasible. Here are some examples:

- Offer adults a variety of online Bible and theology courses for individual study using online courses from colleges and seminaries, video programs on YouTube, online programs and webinars from religious publishers and organizations.

- Provide an online prayer and spirituality center where people can access daily prayer reflections and devotions, offer prayer intentions, pray for others, learn about spiritual practices, download prayer activities for the home, and more.
- Provide an online parent resource center with the best knowledge, practices, and tools for parenting in print, audio, and video; include links to quality parent websites and family faith formation websites and set up a parent blog and/or Facebook page where parents can post their experiences, questions, and insights.
- Provide an online retreat experience available through a publisher or a religious organization.

FAITH FORMATION NETWORKS IN PRACTICE

At this point you are probably wondering, what would a faith formation network for an age group or generation or family look like in practice? Let's review the key design features of a network and then explore how to put them in practice in fashioning a faith formation network.

1. Faith formation is developed around the eight faith-forming processes—caring relationships, celebrating liturgical seasons, celebrating rituals and milestones, learning the Christian tradition and applying it to life, praying and spiritual formation, reading the Bible, serving people in need and working for justice and caring for creation, and worshipping God with the faith community. These eight processes provide both a *framework* for a comprehensive curriculum with age groups, generations, and families and the *content*— knowledge and practices—of the Christian faith.

2. Intergenerational faith formation and whole community faith experiences are at the *center* of all faith formation networks, engaging all ages and generations in the life and events of church life and the Christian faith through participation in intergenerational faith experiences.

3. Age-group and generational faith formation addresses the unique life tasks, needs, interests, and spiritual journeys of people at each stage of life.

4. Family faith formation nurtures family faith, develops the faith life of parents and grandparents, strengthens family life, and builds the parenting knowledge and skills of parents.

5. Missional faith formation expands and extends the church's presence through outreach, connection, relationship building, and engagement with people where they live; and provides pathways for people to consider or reconsider

the Christian faith, to encounter Jesus and the good news, and to live as disciples in a supportive faith community.

6. Faith formation provides a variety of experiences, programs, activities, resources, and social connections that are available anytime and anywhere, in physical places and online spaces, and conducted in variety of settings—self-directed, mentored, at home, in small groups, in large groups, church-wide, in the community, and in the world.

7. Faith formation incorporates formal and informal learning.

8. Faith formation provides the opportunity for personalized and customized learning and faith growth, giving people an active role in shaping their own learning and moving along their own personal trajectories of faith growth. People are guided by trusted mentors/guides who find the right programs, activities, and resources to match with their learning needs.

9. Faith formation recognizes that learning is a process of active inquiry with the initiative residing within the individual. Faith formation networks recognize that the motivation for learning is intrinsic to the person and is driven by a need for autonomy (self-directedness), mastery, and purpose and meaning.

10. Faith formation incorporates digital platforms (websites) that integrate all of the content (programs, activities, resources), connect people to the content and to each other, provides continuity for people across different learning experiences, and is available anytime, anywhere, anyplace, 24x7x365.

11. Faith formation integrates online and face-to-face learning, blending them in a variety of ways from online programs with minimal interaction in physical settings to programs in physical settings that utilize online content or extend the program using online content.

Designing a Network

Imagine designing an Adult Faith Formation Network for adults in their 50s through the early 70s with content that provides developmentally- and generationally-appropriate faith knowledge and practices; engages adults intergenerationally in the life and events of the Christian community; and provides adult programs and activities in a variety of settings and media formats, organized around the eight faith-forming processes and three adult-specific content areas: adult life issues, discovering faith (outreach to the "churchless"), and grandparents.

At the center of the Adult Faith Formation Network is the intergenerational faith community with its events—Sunday worship, the feasts and seasons of the church year, ritual celebrations, acts of justice and service, prayer experiences, spiritual traditions, and the events that originate within the life and history of a individual congregation—and the connections and relationships across generations. It may also have intentional intergenerational programming such as intergenerational learning and service projects. We want to utilize the events of church throughout the Adult Faith Formation Network and encourage adult participation in the life of the faith community and the opportunities for intergenerational connection and relationship.

Programming can be designed and offered in three, four-month seasons: January–April, May–August, and September–December. Here is an example of one season (January–April) that provides a variety of experiences, programs, activities, and resources in physical places and online spaces, and is conducted in variety of settings—self-directed, mentored, at home, in small groups, in large groups, church-wide, in the community, and in the world. (For an illustration of an adult faith formation network and website go to: http://holytrinityadults.weebly.com.) As you read this example of adult faith formation, imagine developing similar networks for every age group in your congregation and for the whole family.

Adult Faith Formation Network

Caring Relationships

- Friday Lent simple meals
- Social gatherings for adults
- Intergenerational experiences and programs in the church community
- Career mentoring program between adults and young adults entering the workplace, addressing work issues, money management, career planning, living as a Christian in the workplace and world, and more

Celebrating the Liturgical Seasons

- A forty-day Lent "curriculum" that connects the Lent events in church life with a variety of activities for experiencing and practicing Lent in daily and home life—delivered online through the congregation's faith formation website, including fasting activities, praying activities, service/almsgiving activities, lectionary reflections, Lent study resources and videos, Lent devotions, and daily Bible readings

Celebrating Rituals and Milestones

- Resources for celebrating adult milestones and life transitions, such as retirement, becoming a grandparent, at home with family and friends

Learning the Christian Tradition and Applying It to Life

- A theology book-of-the-month program with groups meeting at church, at home, in community settings, and online via web conferencing; and online content with discussion questions and links for further learning
- January theology enrichment series: four presentations at church by guest experts on a theological theme; video recording of each presentation for online viewing and small group learning; and online resources for continuing learning
- Online theology courses selected for individual study using offerings at colleges/seminaries and on iTunes University
- An online theology video library of presentations on theological topics for individual or small group study

Praying and Spiritual Formation

- Lent spiritual practices course: a five-session spiritual practices course with sessions on prayer styles and traditions, fixed-hour prayer, contemplation and meditation, spiritual reading and praying with art and music, and Sabbath
- An online Lent retreat experience delivered daily via email

- Online prayer center with links to print, audio, video, and digital resources for daily prayer, devotions, liturgy of the hours, and more

Reading the Bible

- A six-week Lent Bible study program organized in variety of settings with a print resource and online support materials and videos
- Links to online resources for Bible study and a list of Bible apps for individual use

Serving People in Need, Working for Justice, Caring for Creation

- A variety of service/mission projects—just for adults or intergenerational—already offered by justice and service organizations, that provide a range of options for service, e.g., local one-day projects, short-term mission trips of two to five days, weeklong mission trips, and global expedition trips of ten to fourteen days
- An online justice and service center where people can learn about justice issues and the biblical and church teachings on justice, service, and care for creation

Worshipping God within the Faith Community

- Online resources for extending Sunday worship into daily life and family life using a variety of digital content that deepens the understanding and practice of the Sunday readings and sermon, and provides prayer, devotions, rituals, a video of the sermon with a study guide, service/action ideas, conversation activities, and more
- "Coffee and Conversation" groups after Sunday worship to reflect on the Sunday readings using Lectio Divina

Adult Life Issues

- Programs and small groups organized around adult life tasks and issues, such as children getting married, retirement, finances in later life, caring for an aging parent, dealing with illness
- Links to online programs and resources that address adult life tasks and issues, such www.AARP.org
- Connection to programs sponsored by churches or community organizations on adult life issues

Just for Grandparents

- Grandparent-grandchild programs, such as a mini-retreat program, trips, service projects, and more, organized by the church
- Articles and materials to help grandparents understand their role in faith formation and raising their grandchildren
- Faith-forming activities that grandparents can use with their grandchildren
- A list of recommended children's Bibles, storybooks, and video programs that grandparents can use with grandchildren

Discovering Faith

- Sponsor a program, such as Alpha, for "churchless" adults who want to explore the Christian faith again or for the first time
- Develop a weekly program, such as Lifetree Café, in a community setting for adults who want to connect with a community, discuss spiritual matters, and explore faith
- Offer "reentry" experiences and mentors/guides for those who want to join the church community and need a gradual reintroduction to church life and the Christian faith

CONCLUSION

Chapters 2 and 3 have developed the vision for twenty-first century faith formation—a new ecosystem and a network model of faith formation. We now turn toward bringing the vision to life. The next two chapters provide knowledge and skills for designing and implementing a faith formation network. Chapter 4 guides you through a process for designing a faith formation curriculum. Chapter 5 introduces the role of the faith formation curator and the work of curating resources—finding the best resources in all media formats that match with people's learning needs.

Works Cited

Anderson, Keith. "Introducing the Digital Cathedral." (http://pastorkeithanderson.net/item/introducing-the-digital-cathedral#sthash.ViPY5XCd.dpuf)

Anderson, Keith. "The Digital Cathedral: Networked Ministry in a Wireless World." Posted Feb 04, 2014, New Media Project (http://www.cpx.cts.edu/newmedia/blog/new-media-project/2014/02/04/the-digital-cathedral-networked-ministry-in-a-wireless-world#sthash.vj3g6xDW.dpuf)

Anderson, Keith. *The Digital Cathedral: Networked Ministry in a Wireless* World. New York: Morehouse, 2015.

Fuller, Buckminster. "Quotes." (http://www.goodreads.com/author/quotes/165737. Buckminster_Fuller)

Horn, Michael B. and Heather Staker. *Blended: Using Disruptive Innovation to Improve Schools.* San Francisco: Jossey-Bass, 2014.

Ito, Mizuko, Kris Gutierrez, Sonia Livingstone, Bill Penuel, Jean Rhodes, Katie Salie, Juliet Schor, Julian Sefton-Green, and S. Craig Watkins. "Connected Learning: An Agenda for Research and Design." Digital Media and Learning Research Network, 2013. (http://clrn.dmlhub.net)

Pink, Daniel. *Drive: The Surprising Truth About What Motivates Us.* New York: Riverhead, 2009.

Price, Katherine. "Glimpses of the Future of Education." *Building the Future of Education: Museums and the Learning Ecosystem.* Center for the Future of Museums, 2014. (http://www.aam-us.org/docs/default-source/center-for-the-future-of-museums/building-the-future-of-education-museums-and-the-learning-ecosystem.pdf?sfvrsn=2)

"Re-imaging Learning in the 21st Century." MacArthur Foundation: Digital Media and Learning Network, 2010.

Synder, William. "Cultivating Communities." *Faith and Leadership.* July 27, 2008. (http://www.faithandleadership.com/multimedia/william-snyder-cultivating-communities)

Watson, John. "Blending Learning: The Convergence of Online and Face-to-Face Education." National American Council for Online Learning, 2008 (www.inacol.org)

"What Is Blended Learning?" More than Blend Learning. (http://morethanblended.com)

APPENDIX

Connected Learning Principles

(http://clrn.dmlhub.net/publication/connected-learning-an-agenda-for-research-and-design)

In 2013, the Digital Media and Learning Research Network, supported by the MacArthur Foundation, issued a major report, "Connected Learning: An Agenda for Research and Design" that provides a foundation for developing new models of learning for the digital age that are powerful, relevant, and engaging. They describe the concept of *connected learning* as an educational approach designed for our ever-changing world, and to the realities of the digital age where the demand for learning never stops. Connected learning is anchored in research, robust theories of learning, and the best of traditional standards, but also designed to mine the learning potential of the new social media and digital media domains. It harnesses the advances and innovations of our connected age to serve learning.

Connected learning knits together three crucial contexts for learning:

1. **Peer Supported.** In their everyday exchanges with peers and friends, young people are contributing, sharing, and giving feedback in inclusive social experiences that are fluid and highly engaging.

2. **Interest-Powered.** When a subject is personally interesting and relevant, learners achieve much higher-order learning outcomes.

3. **Academically-Oriented.** Learners flourish and realize their potential when they can connect their interests and social engagement to academic studies, civic engagement, and career opportunity.

Core properties of connected learning experiences include:

1. **Production-Centered.** Digital tools provide opportunities for producing and creating a wide variety of media, knowledge, and cultural content in experimental and active ways.

2. **Shared Purpose.** Social media and web-based communities provide unprecedented opportunities for cross-generational and cross-cultural learning and connection to unfold and thrive around common goals and interests.

3. **Openly Networked.** Online platforms and digital tools can make learning resources abundant, accessible, and visible across all learner settings.

Design principles inform the intentional connecting of learning environments:

1. **Everyone can participate.** Experiences invite participation and provide many different ways for individuals and groups to contribute.

2. **Learning happens by doing.** Learning is experiential and part of the pursuit of meaningful activities and projects.

3. **Challenge is constant.** Interest or cultivation of an interest creates both a "need to know" and a "need to share."

4. **Everything is connected.** Young people are provided with multiple learning contexts for engaging in connected learning—contexts in which they receive immediate feedback on progress, have access to tools for planning and reflection, and are given opportunities for mastery.

New media amplifies opportunities for connected learning:

1. **Fostering engagement and self-expression.** Interactive, immersive, and personalized technologies can provide responsive feedback, support a diversity of learning styles and literacy, and pace learning according to individual needs.

2. **Increasing accessibility to knowledge and learning experiences.** Through online search, educational resources, and communities of expertise and interest, young people can easily access information and find relationships that support self-directed and interest-driven learning.

3. **Expanding social supports for interests.** Through social media, young people can form relationships with peers and caring adults that are centered on interests, expertise, and future opportunity in areas of interest.

4. **Expanding diversity and building capacity.** New media networks empower marginalized and non-institutionalized groups and cultures to have a voice, mobilize, organize, and build capacity.

CHAPTER 4

REIMAGINING THE CURRICULUM

When we think about curriculum our thoughts often focus on *choosing* a curriculum, which means purchasing a resource—an age-graded or life-stage series of "textbooks" (in print or digital versions). Equating curriculum with a printed text series is a product of the schooling approach to curriculum. We also tend to associate curriculum with children and teens—because of the predominance of Sunday school. Rarely do we talk about a lifelong formation curriculum or an adult curriculum or a family curriculum.

We need to rethink what a faith formation curriculum means today and move beyond a reliance on a linear, sequential, grade-level curriculum approach, dominated by printed texts that serve as the "curriculum" and are developed primarily for use in a classroom or age-group centered setting at church. This approach to curriculum is simply not up to the challenges of the twenty-first century!

The word *curriculum* is derived from the Latin verb *currere*, which means to run. In literal terms, a curriculum is a course to be run; it is a *journey*. A faith formation curriculum is a lifelong journey of discipleship—a process of experiencing, learning, and practicing the Christian faith as we seek to follow Jesus and his way in today's world.

If we imagine a faith formation curriculum as a lifelong journey of growing in faith and discipleship, then we can think of curriculum as the subject matter and processes that engage people in learning, experiencing, and practicing the Christian faith along this journey. We can think of curriculum as the life, the substance that is experienced. And this life—this substance—is greatly expanded both in content and in learning environments in the twenty-first century.

PART I. ESSENTIAL FEATURES

How should we envision a lifelong faith formation curriculum in the twenty-first century—a curriculum that reflects our continuing mission, the new faith formation ecosystem, and a contemporary approach to learning?

I am proposing eight essential features of a twenty-first century curriculum that move us from theory and vision to curriculum and practice. Reflected in these eight characteristics are the foundational insights we explored in Chapters 2 and 3. A faith formation curriculum for the twenty-first century is:

1. **Holistic.** Envisioning Christian faith as a way of the head, the heart, and the hands—informing, forming, and transforming people in Christian faith and identity.

2. **Comprehensive and balanced.** Developed around the eight primary faith-forming processes that facilitate faith growth and incorporate essential knowledge and practices of the Christian faith: caring relationships, celebrating liturgical seasons, celebrating rituals and milestones, learning the Christian tradition and applying it to life, praying and spiritual formation, reading the Bible, serving people in need and working for justice and caring for creation, and worshipping God with the faith community.

3. **Systemic.** Providing a curriculum for the new faith-forming ecosystem—an intergenerational faith formation curriculum centered in church life and events, an age-group and generational faith formation curriculum, a family faith formation curriculum for the home, and a missional faith formation curriculum for the spiritual but not religious and the unaffiliated.

4. **Lifelong.** Spanning ten decades of life and addressing the uniqueness of each stage of life.

5. **Contextual.** Addressing the needs, hungers, interests, and concerns of people today, and their unique spiritual and faith journeys by embracing an approach that moves from life to faith to life.

6. **Digitally enabled.** Complementing the gathered community settings with online learning environments and utilizing the abundance of digital media and tools for learning and faith formation.

7. **Connected.** Linking church life, age groups/generations, daily/home life, and online life through continuous faith formation—connecting participation in church life and events with daily/home life by using online content and connections *or* reaching people at home and in daily life with online faith formation content and experiences that connect to church life and events.

8. **Multi-platform.** Delivered and conducted in multiple settings—self-directed,

mentored, at home, in small groups, in large groups, church-wide, in the community and world, and in physical and online learning environments.

The Curriculum of Lifelong Faith Formation

How can we design a lifelong faith formation curriculum for the twenty-first century that embodies the eight features described above?

A lifelong faith formation curriculum is really an integration of four curricula: intergenerational, age group, family, and missional—all supported by digitally-enabled, online faith formation.

Intergenerational Faith Formation

Central to twenty-first century faith formation is guided participation in a community of practice. Joyce Mercer makes the key point that this is not just "doing." It includes fully and actively practicing our faith in everyday life and making theological meaning out of the stuff of everyday life. Theological themes and faith practices are embedded in the experience of church life throughout the year and are an integral element of the curriculum. For example:

- *The feasts and seasons of the church year* provide a natural rhythm and calendar to the curriculum: Advent and Christmas seasons, Epiphany, Baptism of the Lord, Call of the Disciples, Ash Wednesday, Lenten season, Holy Week, Easter, Easter season, Pentecost, All Saints and All Souls, and remembrances of saints and holy people throughout the year.
- The *Revised Common and Catholic Lectionaries* provide a rich curriculum for the whole community with its three-year cycle of weekly readings from the Old Testament, psalms, epistles, and gospels built around the seasons of the church year. The *Narrative Lectionary* is a four-year cycle of readings from September through May each year following the sweep of the biblical story, from creation through the early Christian church.
- *Ritual, milestone, and sacramental celebrations* provide events rich in theological meaning and faith practice that celebrate the faith journey throughout life: baptism, confirmation, first Bible, first communion, graduation, marriage, funerals, and much more.
- *Acts of service and justice*—locally and globally—provide a focus on mission to the world and put in action biblical and church teachings on service, justice, and care for the earth.

When the experiences of church life are the focus of intergenerational and age-group learning, we have the opportunity to *prepare* people—with the appropriate knowledge and practices—for participation in the central events of church life and the Christian faith, and to *guide* their participation and reflection upon those events.

Use the following template to develop a profile of the events and activities of the congregation. Produce the profile on newsprint, in a written report, and/or on an Excel spreadsheet.

Faith-forming Processes	Church Life and Events
Caring relationships	
Celebrating the liturgical seasons	
Celebrating rituals and milestones	
Learning the Christian tradition	
Praying and spiritual formation	
Reading the Bible	
Serving people in need, working for justice, caring for creation	
Worshipping God	

Age-group and Generational Faith Formation

Age-group and generational faith formation addresses the unique life tasks, needs, interests, and spiritual journeys of age groups and generations across the whole life span. The eight faith-forming processes are the framework for an age-specific or generationally-specific curriculum, which also includes life issues appropriate to that stage of life and missional initiatives to engage the spiritual but not religious and the unaffiliated and uninterested.

Age-group and generation faith formation needs to be connected to the events of church life and to family life. For example:

- People learn about worship and how to worship; experience Sunday worship with the faith community and practice worshipping; and live the Sunday worship experience at home and in their daily lives.
- People learn about the Bible and how to read it, interpret it, and apply it to their lives; experience the Bible at Sunday worship and at home; and develop their own practice of Bible study and reading.
- People learn about Jesus and the Christian tradition—teachings, history, practices, what it means for life today, and how to live the Christian faith today; and experience the life of Jesus and the Christian tradition through participation in the events of church life, especially church year feasts and seasons.

- People learn about prayer and spirituality, and how to develop their spiritual lives through prayer and spiritual discipleship; experience the prayer life of the faith community; and develop their own practice of prayer and the spiritual disciplines.
- People learn about the justice issues of our day and the biblical and church teachings on justice, service, and care for creation; experience acts of justice and service with the faith community—locally and globally; and engage in the practices of serving those in need, caring for creation, and working for justice—as individuals, with their families, and with their church and other groups and organizations.

Use the following template to develop a profile of age-group/generational programming and the (potential) connection to the life and events of the church. Produce the profile on newsprint, in a written report, and/or on a Excel spreadsheet.

Faith-forming Processes	Age-group/ Generational Programming	Connection to Church Life and Events
Caring relationships: intergenerational and peer relationships, supportive communities		
Celebrating the liturgical seasons: feasts and seasons of the church year		
Celebrating rituals and milestones: celebrating rituals, sacraments, and milestones at significant moments in one's life journey and faith journey		
Reading the Bible: studying and interpreting the Bible—its message, its meaning, and its application to life today		
Learning the Christian tradition: learning the content of the tradition (Trinity, Jesus, church, beliefs, morality, and ethics), reflecting upon that content, integrating it into one's faith life, applying it to life today, and living its meaning in the world		
Praying, devotions, and spiritual formation: personal and communal prayer; being formed by the spiritual disciplines		
Serving and justice: living the Christian mission in the world—engaging in service to those in need, care for God's creation, and action and advocacy for justice		
Worshipping God with the faith community: experiencing God's living presence through Scripture, preaching, and Eucharist; and being sent forth on mission		

Family Faith Formation

Congregations equip families to become centers of learning and faith growth at home by nurturing family faith and developing the faith life of parents and grandparents, strengthening family life by focusing on family asset-building, and developing the knowledge, skills, and confidence of parents (and grandparents) for parenting. There are five elements in a family faith formation curriculum for the home:

- *Nurturing family faith at home* by utilizing the eight faith-forming processes as the primary content—knowledge, experiences, practices, and resources—developed from events of church life, as well as specially designed family resources.
- *Building strong families* by developing family assets: 1) nurturing relationships (positive communication, affection, emotional openness, encouragement for pursuing talents and interests); 2) establishing routines (family meals, shared activities, meaningful traditions—holidays, rituals, celebrations, dependability); 3) maintaining expectations (openness about tough topics, fair rules, defined boundaries, clear expectations, contributions to family); 4) adapting to challenges (management of daily commitments, adaptability problem-solving, democratic decision-making); and 5) connecting to the community (neighborhood cohesion, relationship with others in the community, participating in enriching activities, supportive resources in the community (*The American Family Asset Study*, Search Institute).
- *Parent faith formation* through participation in intergenerational faith formation at church and church life, and through targeted programs of theological and biblical formation for parents and grandparents.
- *Parenting for faith-growth training* to equip parents with knowledge, skills, and resources to develop the faith life of their children and practice faith at home as a family.
- *Parenting education* that develops the knowledge, skills, and confidence of parents (and grandparents) for parenting children and teens, with a special focus on parent practices, such as love and affection, stress management, relationship skills, respect, promoting and modeling learning, life skills, behavior management, healthy lifestyle, supporting spiritual and religious development and practice, and protection and safety.

Use the following template to develop a profile of current and potential family programming and the (potential) connection to the life and events of the church. Produce the profile on newsprint, in a written report, and/or on a Excel spreadsheet.

Content Areas	Programs, Activities, and Resources for the Home	Connection to Church Life and Events
Faith practices • Celebrating the liturgical seasons • Celebrating rituals and milestones • Learning the Christian tradition • Praying • Reading the Bible • Serving, working for justice, caring for creation		
Family Assets • Nurturing relationships • Establishing routines • Maintaining expectations • Adapting to challenges • Connecting to the community		
Parent faith formation		
Parenting for faith-growth training		
Parenting education		

Missional Faith Formation

The mission curriculum includes two types of "content." The first involves expanding and extending the church's presence through outreach, connection, relationship building, and engagement with people where they live—engaging with people around their life situation (needs, interests, concerns), their quest for meaning and purpose in life, their drive to make a difference in world and in lives of others, and more. This first type of missional curriculum provides a safe environment for people to explore life-centered and spiritual-centered activities. (See the missional section on page 50 in Chapter 2 for more ideas.)

The second type of curriculum content provides pathways for people to consider or reconsider the Christian faith, to encounter Jesus and the good news, and to live as disciples in a supportive faith community. Missional faith formation guides people as they move from discovery to exploration to commitment. The catechumenal process with its ritual stages and formational content—participation in the life of the faith community, education in Scripture and the Christian tradition, apprenticeship in the Christian life, intimate connection with the liturgy and rituals of the church, moral formation, development of a life of prayer, and engagement in actions of justice and service. Programs like *The Alpha Course* cover the basics of Christianity in a multisession course in a supportive small group environment.

Use the following template to develop a profile of current and potential missional activities in two categories: outreach and pathways. Produce the profile on newsprint, in a written report, and/or on a Excel spreadsheet.

Target Audience	Expanding and Extending the Church's Presence through Outreach and Community	Pathways to Jesus, Discipleship, and the Christian Faith

Online Faith Formation

Digital media and the online environment provide the means to connect church life, age groups/generations, and daily/home life through continuous faith formation—connecting participation in church life and events with daily/home life by using online content and connections *or* reaching people at home and in daily life with online faith formation content and experiences that connect to church life and events. For example:

- Extend and deepen people's experience and participation in church events and programs with online content for daily and home life. Consider the possibilities for extending Sunday worship, church year feasts and seasons, intergenerational and family programs, classes, youth meetings, mission trips, retreat experiences, vacation Bible school, and more.

- Provide a complete faith formation experience online connected to the life of the church, for example, a forty-day Lent "curriculum" that connects the Lent events at church with online content for experiencing and practicing Lent in daily and home life. For example:

CHURCH LIFE EVENTS	DAILY AND HOME LIFE ACTIVITIES
Ash Wednesday	Fasting activities
Lent Sunday liturgies	Praying activities
Stations of the Cross	Service/almsgiving activities
Lent prayer	Lectionary reflections
Lent retreat	Lent study resources and videos
Lent service	Lent devotions
Lent soup suppers	Daily Bible readings

- "Flip the classroom or program" by creating a digital platform to provide the content that people would learn in the gathered setting into an online learning space using print, audio, video, and more. And then transform the gathered program using interactive activities, discussion, project-based learning, and practice and demonstration. One example is redesigning children's faith formation so that children and their parents are learning online at home and doing activities together, and then refocusing "class time" to engage children in creating projects and activities that demonstrate their learning. Another example is designing a high school confirmation program that provides the content that used to be taught in the weekly sessions in an online platform for individual learning—watching videos, reading short materials, and writing a reflection journals; engages the young people in small groups during the month to discuss their online learning; and then meets monthly in a large group gathered session for discussion, interactive activities, and application of the content to living as a Christian today. During the year retreats, worship, and service projects offer additional gathered sessions.
- Offer opportunities for individuals, families, and small groups to utilize the digital platform as their primary learning setting and provide opportunities for regular interaction in face-to-face, gathered settings or in a web conference format, such as a Google+ Hangout. One example is offering six, one-hour parent webinar programs delivered to parents at home in four-month semesters: three webinars followed by a parent gathering at church; three more webinars and concluding with a parent gathering at church. Another example is developing an online Bible study where groups can meet regularly in a physical setting or virtually through Skype or a Google+ Hangout for sharing their learning.

- Provide high-quality and easily accessible online religious content—courses, activities, print and e-books, audio and video programs, and content-rich websites—on the faith formation website or with links to select websites. One example is offering adults a variety of online Bible and theology courses for individual study using online courses from colleges and seminaries, video programs on YouTube, and online programs and webinars from religious publishers and organizations. Another example is providing an online prayer and spirituality center where people can access daily prayer reflections and devotions, offer prayer intentions, pray for others, learn about spiritual practices, download prayer activities for the home, and more.

The chart on the next page reflects the understanding of curriculum just presented. Consider using this tool as a way to assess your current approach to curriculum and as a guide to expanding your faith formation curriculum.

A Lifelong Curriculum Plan

The subject matter and processes that engage people in learning, experiencing, and practicing the Christian faith

Content Areas	Church Life & Events	Family at Home	Children & Parents	Youth & Parents	Young Adults	Mid-life Adults	Mature Adults	Older Adults	Digital & Online
Caring relationships									
Celebrating the liturgical seasons									
Celebrating rituals and milestones									
Learning the Christian tradition and applying it to life									
Praying and spiritual formation									
Reading the Bible									
Serving people in need, working for justice, caring for creation									
Worshipping God within the faith community									
Life stage • Individual • Family assets • Parents									
Missional activities • Outreach • Pathways									

PART 2. REIMAGING CURRICULUM DESIGN

In the twenty-first century, the curriculum is the network. On the network people can experience the life and substance of the Christian faith in a way that expands both the content and environments and can be personalized and customized. The fundamental operating system and delivery system for faith formation is now the *network*.

- The network provides a variety of experiences, programs, activities, resources, and social connections that are available anytime and anywhere, in physical places and online spaces, and conducted in variety of settings— self-directed, mentored, at home, in small groups, in large groups, church- wide, in the community, and in the world.
- The network incorporates digital platforms (websites) that integrate all of the content (programs, activities, resources), connect people to the content and to each other, provide continuity for people across different learning experiences, and is available anytime, anywhere.
- The network integrates online and face-to-face learning, blending learning in a variety of ways from online programs with minimal interaction in physical settings to programs in physical settings that utilize online content or extend the program using online content.

How can we design a curriculum that is holistic, comprehensive, systemic, life- long, contextual, digitally enabled, connected, and multi-platform? The following design process will help bring these characteristics to life in a curriculum plan and a network design that reflects a twenty-first century approach to faith formation.

Step 1. Research your target audience and identify needs
Step 2. Build the faith formation network design
Step 3. Generate programming for the faith formation network
Step 4. Design a season of faith formation programming
Step 5. Build the digital platform—a faith formation website
Step 6. Design a process for assessing and personalizing learning
Step 7. Test the seasonal plan and web design
Step 8. Launch the faith formation network
Step 9. Evaluate the season of programming
Step 10. Design the new season of programming

Ideas for designing programming (intergenerational, age group, family, and missional) can be found at http://www.21stCenturyFaithFormation.com and http://www.IntergenerationalFaith.com. The 21st Century Faith Formation web- site has a variety of strategies for (digitally) blended faith formation.

Preparation

First, develop a *network team* (or task force) to design your network for a target audience: age group, generation, or families. The task force should include church staff and ministry leadership, faith formation leaders, and members from your target audience who can bring new perspectives and experiences to the design work. It is very helpful to have several people who bring experience and expertise in the digital technologies and media, and social media. The task force will need a facilitator. Prepare the team by having them read Chapters 1–3 in this book.

Second, identify the *target audience* for your faith formation network, for example: children and families, adolescents and families; young adults (20s–30s), mid-life adults (40s–50s), mature adults (mid 60s–70s), and older adults (75+), multi-generational family, and more. You can adapt these categories by grouping several categories, such as all adults 30 and over or children and adolescents; or by focusing more narrowly, such as young children and parents, 0–5 years old. Note: The design process in this chapter is written for designing a network and digital platform for an age group or family. This process can be applied to the whole faith community—something more suitable for smaller size churches or for congregations that want to develop an all-ages network around their intergenerational events and ministries.

Third, complete the four profile forms in Part 1 of this chapter for intergenerational, age-group, family, and missional faith formation. This information will provide a starting point for designing the faith formation network in Step 3.

Step 1. Research Your Target Audience and Identify Needs

Conduct research on the target audience using the following categories:

- life-stage issues (developmental needs, concerns, interests)
- generational issues
- milestones and life transitions
- ethnic and cultural needs
- spiritual and religious needs

By consulting research findings and listening carefully to people in the community, the team can determine the most important needs a faith formation network should address through programs, activities, and resources. Follow these guidelines for effective research.

Review relevant research and effective faith formation practices for the target audience. Begin with existing research studies on the spiritual and religious needs, interests, and life tasks of your target audience to identify important themes to address. Review research and case studies of effective practices to determine what's most effective in faith formation with the target audience. Consult the research reports and effective practice articles online in the "Library" of the Faith Formation Learning Exchange: www.faithformationlearningexchange. net, and at www.21stCenturyFaithFormation.com.

Consider the following questions to guide the research:

1. *Life Stage.* What's happening in the lives and world of your target audience today: family, work, leisure, relationships, sexuality, suffering and grief, social and political issues, community issues? What are the developmental life tasks of people in your target audience?

2. *Generational.* What is the generational identity and the unique generational characteristics of your target audience (builders, boomers, Gen X, millennials, iGeneration)?

3. *Milestones and Transitions.* What are the significant milestones and transitions in the lives of your target audience? (For example: marriages, births, graduations, geographic relocations, family formation and re-formation, career changes, empty nests, retirement, unanticipated illness, divorce, and the loss of loved ones.)

4. *Ethnic/Cultural Needs.* Which ethnic/cultural communities and traditions are present in your target audience? What are the unique lived experiences, needs, and aspirations of people from each ethnic/cultural community?

5. *Spiritual and Religious Needs.* What are the significant spiritual and religious needs, interests, and concerns of people in your target audience?

Conduct focus group research with the target audience. An excellent way to gather information about people in the community is through focus groups. Organize focus groups of eight to twelve people in the target audience. Select a diversity of people in each focus group, reflecting ethnic/cultural diversity, socio-economic diversity, and spiritual and religious diversity (from the actively engaged to the "churchless"). Meet for about one hour in a variety of locations and times. Remember that people who are not involved in church may be hesitant to come to a meeting at church. Have two people lead each focus group—one to record (on a computer or tablet is preferable) and one to ask the questions. The recorder can also ask follow-up questions as appropriate. Use the following questions as a guide for developing focus group interviews. Every focus group needs to use the same questions so that comparisons can be made across the groups. In a 60-minute focus group there is usually time for at least seven questions that you can select from the following list.

1. How would you describe your age group in key words or phrases?

2. What are some of the key life tasks that your age group is experiencing?

3. What are some of the important life issues that your age group is experiencing today?

4. What are the most meaningful experiences you have in life? What makes these experiences meaningful to you?

5. How important is your relationship with God? Why?

6. Where do you experience God most?

7. What are the significant spiritual issues that your age group is experiencing today?

8. What is most important to you about being a Christian (or a member of a particular denomination or faith tradition) today?

9. How do you live your Christian faith? Name some of the ways you put your faith into practice.

10. How can the church help you to continue growing as a Christian? Be specific. Name some of the things you would like to see your church offer for your age group.

Compile the results from focus groups by identifying patterns or recurring themes about the life tasks and spiritual and religious needs. Also pay attention to information that may be unique to one focus group. Sometimes this uncovers important insights about the target audience.

Conduct observation of the target audience in the community. Engage the team in becoming anthropologists by observing people in the community. Develop an observation checklist and ask team members to spend a week simply observing people at work, at school, at play, at stores, in coffee shops and restaurants, and so on. Watch for things like:

1. What are some of the most popular activities in the community?

2. Where do people gather outside of work and school—coffee shop, gym, mall, park, community center, YMCA/YWCA, and so on? What are they doing there?

3. Where do people work? Do most people work in the community or do they commute to another area? What types of jobs do people have?

4. What are the most popular or well-attended churches in the community?

5. Where are people on Sunday morning, if they are not at worship?

Find patterns in the research findings. An "Empathy Map," developed by the Stanford School of Design, is one tool to synthesize observations and draw out insights from the research. Organize research findings into the following four quadrants: What are people saying, doing, thinking, and feeling? Do this activity as a research team and use one or more sheets of newsprint to compile the findings.

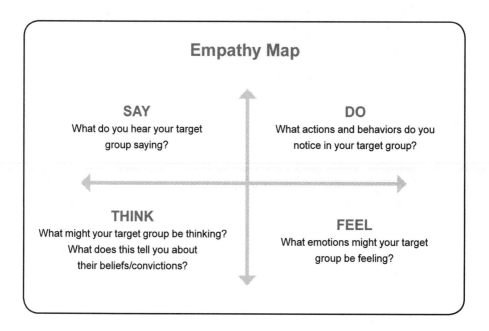

Review the results of the Empathy Map and identify the most important *needs, interests, issues,* and *concerns* of the target audience using the categories below. Record them on newsprint or create a report for everyone.

- life stage issues (developmental needs, concerns, interests)
- generational issues
- milestones and life transitions
- ethnic and cultural needs
- spiritual and religious needs

Step 2. Build the Faith Formation Network Design

Begin building the faith formation network by determining the content areas appropriate for the target audience. Use the eight faith-forming processes as the basic framework for the network. The eight processes can be combined, as in the Families with Children Network example on page 101. New content areas can be added to the network (perhaps some surfaced in the research).

- life issues
- reaching the "churchless"
- life-stage role such as parents in a families with children network or grandparents in an adult network
- major programs such as children's programming in families with children network or confirmation program for an adolescent network

Diagram your network on a sheet of newsprint. Be comprehensive even if it looks overwhelming. You can always combine content areas or modify them later in the process. Examples on pages 100–102 illustrate three faith formation network designs.

Building a Faith Formation Network

FOUNDATIONAL CONTENT AREAS

1. **Caring relationships**
2. **Celebrating the liturgical seasons**
3. **Celebrating rituals and milestones**
4. **Learning the Christian tradition and applying it to life**
5. **Praying and spiritual formation**
6. **Reading the Bible**
7. **Serving people in need, working for justice, caring for creation**
8. **Worshipping God within the faith community**
9. **Life issues**
10. **Missional**
11. **Life stage**
12. **Major programs**

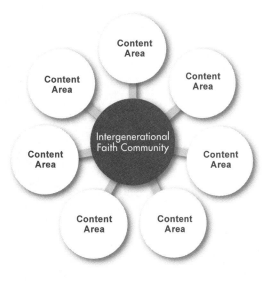

Example: Whole Community Faith Network

The Whole Community Network illustrates how a smaller-sized church can develop one faith formation network for all ages. At the center of the network is the life and events of the intergenerational faith community. Smaller-sized churches can focus their energy intergenerationally by engaging all ages in the life and events of church life—Sunday worship, church year feasts and seasons, mission and service, caring relationships, prayer—and developing intergenerational learning programs around these events.

Each life stage would have content (programs, activities, and resources) that applies the intergenerational experiences and learning to their lives in age-appropriate ways, as well as content that addresses age-appropriate religious and spiritual needs, and life-stage needs, concerns, and interests. The twelve foundational content areas (page 99) provide the basic framework for these life-stage networks. To reduce the complexity of the network these content areas can be combined, for example, a faith practices category that includes several foundational content areas.

Example: Families with Children Network

The Families with Children Faith Formation Network combines several of the eight faith-forming processes together and adds a content area for family assets, a life-stage role for parents, and a program area for children's programming.

Example: Adult Faith Formation Network
(Adults in their 50s–mid 70s)

The Adult Faith Formation Network incorporates the eight faith-forming processes, combines celebrating rituals and milestones with adult life issues because of similar content, adds missional, life issues, and a life-stage role for grandparents.

Step 3. Generate Programming for the Faith Formation Network

With the network design set, programming can be added to each content area. Use the following process to generate programming ideas for each content area of the network. Generate a list of all the possible programs, activities, and resources that *could* be included in the network. This list becomes the database of ideas that can be used to develop each season of program for the network. The following template provides a format for adding programming to each network content area.

1. Correlate the most important needs from the research into the appropriate content areas of the network. Some of the important needs will be included in multiple content areas.

2. Add the faith formation programs that will continue to be offered for the target audience into the appropriate content areas of the network. Some programs may be listed more than once. (See the completed profile forms from Part 1.)

3. Add events, ministries, and programs from the intergenerational faith community into the appropriate content areas of the network. Some events/programs may be listed more than once. (See the completed profile form from Part 1.)

Use a large newsprint sheet to record information and to see the whole picture of network programming.

Target Audience:				
Network content areas	**Important needs for research from this content area**	**Current programming in this content area**	**Intergenerational events/programs that connect to this content area**	**New program ideas for this area**

It would also be easy to create an Excel spreadsheet with all of this information. Once you have generated program ideas for various content areas you can follow these steps.

Review the profile of programming. Begin by analyzing the current age-specific and intergenerational programming using the following questions:

1. What needs are we *not* currently addressing in this target audience?

2. Who are we currently serving? Who are we *not* serving? Do we have outreach and programming directed toward the "churchless"—the spiritual but not religious and the unaffiliated and uninterested?

3. Do we have strong intergenerational connections and programming for this target audience?

4. Are we utilizing online/digital programming and resources with this target audience?

5. Do we have a variety of learning environments for this target audience: self-directed, mentored, at home, in small groups, in large groups, church-wide, in the community, and in the world?

Identify opportunities for blended faith formation. Use the Blended Faith Formation Continuum that follows to review current programming and intergenerational connections to discover ways to use the blended faith formation strategies in redesigning existing programming or develop new programming with online and digital strategies.

Digital media and the online environment provide the means to connect church life, age groups/generations, and daily/home life through continuous faith formation—connecting participation in church life and events with daily/home life by using online content and connections *or* reaching people at home and in daily life with online faith formation content and experiences that connect to church life and events.

Digital media and the online environment provide the means to redesign a gathered program by "flipping the program"—providing online content for individual or small group study and then gathering to discuss, apply, practice, and demonstrate learning.

Blended Faith Formation Continuum

ONLINE ⟵⟶ FACE-TO-FACE

Fully Online	Mostly Online	Online & Gathered	Gathered & Online Content	Gathered with Online Content
An online program with all learning done online and limited face-to-face, gathered learning settings	A mostly online program with opportunities for regular interaction in face-to-face, gathered settings	Online learning focused on presenting the content of the program *combined with* face-to-face, gathered sessions using active learning methods to discuss, practice, and apply the content	A gathered event or program that provides online content and activities to extend and expand the learning from the gathered program	A gathered event or program that uses online content as part of the design of the event or program

For more information on blended faith formation see the examples in Chapter 3 on page 70. For resources and ideas for blended faith formation go to www.21stCenturyFaithFormation.com.

Generate ideas. Generate ideas for new programming for each content area on the network. Remember that programs can be conducted in online spaces and physical places; in a variety of settings: on your own (self-directed), mentored, at home, in small groups, in large groups, church-wide, in the community, and in the world; and with a variety of programs, activities, and resources—print, audio, video, and digital/online.

New programming ideas can be intergenerational as well as age specific. First, determine if any current age-specific programs can be redesigned to become intergenerational experiences. Second, identify new programs that are built around intergenerational events and programs, such as learning programs that prepare people—with the appropriate knowledge and practices—for participating in the central events of church life and guide their participation and reflection upon those events.

Together as a team generate new ideas for programming across the content areas of the network. Begin by consulting the ideas for intergenerational, family, missional, digital/online programming at www.21stCenturyFaithFormation.com and www.IntergenerationalFaith.com.

Use the following questions to help you generate ideas. Record the ideas on newsprint for all to see.

1. What new programming do we need to offer to address the needs that surfaced in our research?

2. What would our target audience like to see the church offer them through faith formation?

3. How can we address the audience's needs through age-specific programming?

4. How can we address the audience's needs through intergenerational or family programming?

5. How can we develop missional outreach programming and strategies to reach the "churchless" in our target audience?

Here are two activities that provide a creative alternative to simple brainstorming.

"What If" You Used Your Imagination?

Use imagination to generate ideas. The easiest way to begin is by saying: "I need fresh and novel ideas to solve my challenge. I will suspend all judgment and see what free and easy ideas we can think up. It doesn't matter how weird or offbeat they are." Allow your team the freedom to conceptualize without judging ideas in terms of the real world. Ask team members to list as many "what if" statements as they can on Post-it® notes (for example, "What if we developed a community café to reach people who are spiritual, but not involved in the church community?"). Ask them to complete the "What if…" statement personally, writing one statement per Post-it. After several minutes, ask people to place their Post-it notes on a sheet of easel paper. Then cluster similar ideas together. When ideas are grouped based on common characteristics or themes, an organization and structure begins to arise from the information. More ideas are generated as people begin to see the structure and fill in the gaps. A sense of priority is often revealed as one or more of the clusters claim the energy and interest of the group.

"How Might We?"

Brainstorm responses to the question: "How Might We?" Distribute Post-it® notes and pens/markers to everyone on the team. Ask them to start their opportunity statements with "How Might We . . . " and abbreviate on post-its with "HMW." Go for quantity, not quality at this point. Post all of the ideas on sheets of easel paper. Cluster similar HMW statements.

Compile a complete report. Use the template that follows to compile a report of the results. This report presents all of the ideas from which seasonal plans can be designed: January–April, May–August, and September–December.

Target Audience:				
Network content areas	Important needs for research from this content area	Current programming in this content area	Intergenerational events/programs that connect to this content area	New program ideas for this area

Step 4. Design a Season of Faith Formation Programming

The most manageable way to program a faith formation network is to develop a three-season approach: January–April, May–August, and September–December. This means launching new programming three times a year and completely updating your website three times a year with the new programming as well as recurring programming. (For an example of a season of programming for adults see Chapter 3. For an illustration of an adult network and website go to: http://holytrinityadults. weebly.com; and for families with children network go to http://holytrinityfamilies. weebly.com.)

All of the network content areas do not need to be introduced in the first season of programming. Over the course of a year (three seasons) network content areas and programming can be added so that the complete plan is finally implemented in the fourth season. Some of the programming will be consistent in every season, while other programming will be specific to a season. Programming from a completed season is archived online (on the website) so that it can be reused in another season or reintroduced a year later.

Here is a guide to developing one season of programming. Develop a first draft of the season and then review all of the programming and make final choices about what to include in the season. Use the template that follows and record the information on newsprint sheets to get a overall view of the season.

Seasonal Plan				
Network Content Area	**Programming & Dates**			
	Month 1	Month 2	Month 3	Month 4

First, identify the season: January 1–May 1 or May 1–September 1 or September 1–January 1.

Second, add continuing age-group programs to the seasonal plan. Use the seasonal plan template to record the results: list the network content areas and then add the programs to the appropriate month.

Third, add intergenerational events and programs from the faith community to the seasonal plan. Explore the possibility of redesigning current age-specific programs to become intergenerational experiences. Explore the possibility of designing new programs that are built around intergenerational events and programs. (For more ideas go to www.IntergenerationalFaith.com.) Add redesigned or new programming to the seasonal plan.

Fourth, explore the possibility of redesigning existing programming by adding a digital blended strategy, such as adding digital content to extend a program, or "flipping" the program, or offering the program in multiple learning environments, such as video recording a presentation to offer it online as a self-study or small group study or offering the same program as in a large group format or small group format. (See the blended faith formation ideas in Chapter 3 on page 70.) Add redesigned or new programming to the Seasonal Plan.

Fifth, review all of the new age-specific programs and intergenerational events/programs generated in Design Step 3. Select new program ideas to introduce in this season. Use the seasonal plan template to record the results: list the content areas and then add the programs to the appropriate month.

Try to provide programs in *different learning environments* and/or one program in multiple learning environments: on your own (self-directed), with a mentor, at home, in small groups, in large groups, in the congregation, in the community, in the world.

Try to implement a program idea with a *blended (digital) faith formation* strategy: gathered program with online content, gathered program and online content, online and gathered in one program, mostly online, and fully online.

Sixth, develop the final version of the seasonal plan. Select the program ideas for each network content area. Some content areas may have too many programs to launch in one season. Select the ones that will be included in this season and save the other program ideas for another season.

Schedule programming in each network content area. Some of the programming flows through multiple months in a season, such as a weekly Bible study group or children's program. Some programs are monthly, such as a monthly webinar for parents. Other programs are seasonal—Advent, Christmas, Lent, and Easter—and therefore anchored in one or more months. Still other programming/resources are always available, such as an online course or a video program or Bible study resources.

One way to manage the variety of programming is to focus on one month of major programming in the network content areas. For example the "Learning the Tradition" content area might select one month to schedule its theology enrichment series with four presentations from guest experts and options for small group study and online study using the video recordings. The Bible area might focus its programming in a different month, perhaps around a church year season, such as Lent. This approach reduces the overlap among major programming and helps people participate in multiple experiences. See the example of adult and family learning pages in Step 5. (For an online example of this monthly approach view http://holytrinityadults.weebly.com, and http://holytrinityfamilies.weebly.com.)

Final Plan for the Season

Network Content Area	Programming & Dates			
	Month 1	Month 2	Month 3	Month 4

Lastly, develop specific plans for each program. Include the following information:

- Date or month
- Learning environment(s)
- Digital strategy(s)
- Resources
- Leaders
- Cost

Step 5. Build the Digital Platform— A Faith Formation Website

Building a digital platform (website) is essential to the network approach to faith formation.

This digital platform provides the primary way to connect people to the network's offerings and to connect people with each other. A faith formation website provides the platform for publishing and delivering the experiences, content, programs, activities, and resources of the network. A website provides the platform for *seamless* learning across a variety of experiences, resources, locations, times, or settings. The website, together with social media, provides continuity between faith formation in the congregation, at home, in daily life, and online. And it is available to people anytime, anywhere, and any device (computer, tablet, smart phone).

It is important to build a website dedicated to faith formation. There can be a website for each target audience and their faith formation network, or a website that integrates several target audiences, such as a family, children, and teens website, or a website for all ages with specific sections for each age group. Most church websites are not equipped for this task. They lack the features, ease of use, capacity, or focus on faith formation to become the digital platform for a network. Today it is much easier to develop a new dedicated website for faith formation and then link it to the church website.

Building a website is made much easier today by the availability of online website builders that provide predesigned website templates, drag-and-drop features to create webpages, and hosting for the website. Three popular website builders to explore are: *Weebly* (www.weebly.com), *Wix* (www.wix.com), and *Squarespace* (www.squarespace.com). All three have easy to use features and very reasonable subscription fees. For advanced users *WordPress* (http://wordpress.org) provides thousands of predesigned templates, lots of customization features, and ready-to-use apps. *WordPress* does require an understanding of web design and some programming ability.

Weebly, *Wix*, and *Squarespace* have detailed tutorials for designing a website. Go to their websites to view the tutorials. There are also independent websites with tutorials and how-to instructions for designing a website, some specific to these three website builders. There are dozens of websites created by *WordPress* users that are dedicated to providing assistance to designers. And, or course, there are YouTube videos that teach the basics of web design and provide particular information for *Weebly*, *Wix*, *Squarespace*, and *WordPress*.

Here are several suggestions for web usability from Steve Krug's excellent and easy-to-use book *Don't Make Me Think: A Common Sense Approach to Web Usability*, Third Edition (Berkeley: New Riders, 2014).

1. Don't make the user think—make web pages self-explanatory so the user hardly has any perceived effort to understand them, for example, clear choice of labels, clearly "clickable" items, simple search.

2. People generally don't read web pages closely; they scan, so design for scanning rather than reading.

3. Create a clear visual hierarchy and menu system (main menu, submenus).

4. Make it very clear how to navigate the site, with clear "signposts" on all pages.

5. Omit needless words.

6. The home page needs the greatest design care to convey site identity and mission.

7. Promote user goodwill by making the typical tasks easy to do, make it easy to recover from errors, and avoid anything likely to irritate users.

While it is beyond the scope of this book to provide step-by-step instructions for designing a website, there are specific features that help customize a website design for the requirements of a network approach to faith formation and the seasonal plan that has been created in Design Step 4.

First, choose a domain name (URL) for the faith formation website. The congregation can either purchase a new domain name for the faith formation website from one of the companies that sell and register domain names or use a free domain name provided by the website builder, e.g., *Weebly* provides hosting and a free website URL with the weebly.com extension, such as http://holytrinityadults.weebly.com.

Second, select a website template that is mobile-responsive, which means that the website will automatically size itself correctly on a computer, laptop, tablet, or phone. The template should do this automatically.

Third, create the primary navigation (main menus) for the website directly from the network content areas. Be sure to select a website template that allows enough room for all of the menu items to be seen. Today's website design favors horizontal menus (running across the webpage), rather than vertical menus (running on the left side of the webpage). Select the template that provides enough room for the menus.

There may be a need to consolidate several content areas of the network to accommodate the website design template. This involves creating submenus (secondary navigation) under the main menu items. Following is an example using the Families with Children Network outlined previously on page 101. The submenu items are listed under the main menu items. Each main menu title would need to adjusted to fit on the webpage.

1. Sunday Worship

2. Seasons of the Year

3. Family Life (Building Family Assets)

4. Family Faith Practices

   • Reading the Bible
   • Learning the Christian Tradition
   • Praying
   • Celebrating Rituals and Milestones
   • Serving, Working for Justice, Caring for Creation

5. Parent Faith Formation and Parenting Education ("Just for Parents")

6. Children's Programming
   (See the example at http://holytrinityfamilies.weebly.com)

Here is an example using the Adult Network outlined previously on page 102, using short titles that will fit across a webpage.

1. Worship

2. Seasons

3. Scripture

4. Spirituality

5. Study

6. Discovering Faith

7. Service

8. Life Issues

9. Grandparents
   (See the example at http://holytrinityadults.weebly.com)

A well-designed site with clear and easy to understand navigation will increase engagement and the time people spend on the website.

Fourth, build each webpage to incorporate all of the programs, activities, and resources for a particular network content area for the seasonal plan. A well-designed site with quality content will increase engagement and create a positive experience for the user—all of which encourage continuous learning.

Each webpage includes content that is uploaded to the website for people to use—audio podcasts, videos, articles, blog posts, interactive features—as well as descriptions and links to programs, activities, and resources that reside on other websites, such as online courses. Webpages can include stable content that is going to be available in every season and seasonal or calendar-specific content.

Each webpage is a "learning page" where people can learn online, download resources, and connect to activities and resources across the web. Here are two examples of webpage design—one for adults and one for parents. For more examples online go to http://holytrinityadults.weebly.com and http://holytrinity families.weebly.com.

Adult Learning Page: November Scripture Enrichment

Focus: Gospel of the New Lectionary Cycle beginning in Advent
Programming:

1. Three-session speaker series on major themes in the gospel: Thursday from 7:30–9:00 pm at the church center.

2. Video presentations of the three sessions online for self study.

3. Video presentations of the three sessions online for small group study with accompanying study guide.

4. Scripture study groups using a four-session introduction to the major themes of the gospel conducted at church, in homes, and in the community.

5. Gospel self-study using links to Scripture websites such as www.enterthebible.org from Luther Seminary.

6. Online course on the gospel with one or more links to existing online courses at a seminary or university or on iTunes U in the Apple iTunes Store.

Family Learning Page: For Parents Only

Focus: Parenting Education
Programming:

1. "First Wednesdays" parent webinar series: 9:00–10:00 pm online with guest presenter. Each month presents a topic of interest for parents, such as positive parenting, communicating well, raising responsible children and teens, celebrating rituals and milestones, and more.

2. "Learn More About. . . ." resources on parenting topics with links to expert websites and videos, such as www.ParentFurther.com from The Search Institute.

3. "Secrets of Happy Families" five-session book group using Bruce Feiler's book of the same name with study groups organized at church, in homes, in a Google+ Hangout, and by parents in self-organized groups. Study group and supportive resources available on the For Parents Only page.

4. Parent videos on a variety of topics available for viewing on the For Parents Only page or with descriptions and links to YouTube or other websites.

5. List of valuable websites and online resources for parents such as the Boys Town Parenting Center with a national hotline just for parents available 24 hours a day (www.boystown.org/parenting).

Fifth, design the website specifically for your target audiences and write the content for them in their language with titles and examples that connect to their lives; select images (photo or short video) that reflect their life situations. Engage the target audience and tell them what they need to know and do.

Be sure to pay careful attention to the titles and descriptions so that they capture people's interests. Develop descriptions that are positive in tone, indicate clearly the content or focus of an activity. Describe how your offerings respond to something within the lives of people. Highlight the relationship between the content and the particular spiritual or religious needs, interests, passions, concerns, or life issues of people. Describe the two to three benefits of engaging in faith formation.

For examples of congregational faith formation websites go to the twenty-first Century Faith Formation website (www.21stCenturyFaithFormation.com) and select the Case Studies section to read articles describing how churches are creating faith formation websites. There are links to dozens of faith formation websites in churches across the United States.

Step 6. Design a Process for Assessing and Personalizing Learning

An important component of a network approach to learning is giving people an active role in shaping their own learning and moving along their own personal trajectories of faith growth. A faith formation network, rich in a diversity of content and a variety of ways to learn, can guide people in creating their own personal learning pathways. Churches can develop processes for helping individuals and families (online and in-person) to:

1. discern learning and faith growth needs

2. work with a mentor or guide to create a plan for faith growth and learning and find resources on the network

3. engage in faith formation experiences

4. reflect on their learning with a mentor/guide or small group

5. identify new needs for growth and learning

A *faith growth learning plan* helps people identify where they are on their spiritual journey, what they need for continuing their growth, who else might share that need, and the resources that could help them meet that need. For example a family faith growth plan could include participating in Sunday worship, developing faith practices at home (daily devotion, Bible reading), celebrating a church year season at home, doing a service project with other families, and more. Congregations provide mentors or guides to assist people in developing their growth plan, accessing the programs and resources that fit their plan, and evaluating their learning.

First, identify people who can serve as mentors or guides to help people discern their learning needs; find the right programs, activities, and resources to match with their learning needs; and assist with the implementation of the faith growth plan.

Second, design a discernment tool, specific to the target audience, to guide people in assessing their learning and faith growth needs. The discernment tool can be used in a group setting with a facilitator, in a one on one setting with a mentor or guide, or in an online setting with instructions for its use and how to find programs, activities, and resources to match with learning needs.

Third, design a faith growth learning plan. Give people a sense of the flow from discerning needs to finding resources on the network to implementing their plan. (For examples of assessment tools and faith growth plans go to www.21stCenturyFaithFormation.com.)

Step 7. Test the Seasonal Plan and Web Design

It's wise to conduct one or two focus group meetings of the target audience to get feedback on the seasonal plan and the usability of the web design. Testing is an opportunity to learn more about the user through observation and engagement. (For insights on testing the web design see Chapter 9, "Usability Testing on 10 Cents a Day," in *Don't Make Me Think: A Common Sense Approach to Web Usability* [Third Edition] by Steve Krug).

Begin by identifying people within the target audience to test the website and give feedback on the seasonal programming. Invite them to a focus group meeting. Use a deliberate procedure when you test. Create a "testing process" so that you can gain important feedback. Here are four suggestions:

1. Let your user experience the network online. Show; don't tell. Let them review the website and the programming. Provide just the minimum context so they understand what to do. (Have computers or tablets available for people to use or ask them to bring a device to the focus group.)

2. Have them talk through their experience. For example, when appropriate, ask "Tell me what you are thinking as you are doing this."

3. Actively observe. Watch how they use (and misuse!) the website. Don't immediately "correct" what your user is doing.

4. Follow up with questions, such as: "Show me why this would (or would not) work for you." "Can you tell me more about how this made you feel?" "Why?" "Do you find things that interest you and connect with your life?" "Are there things you would have liked to see?"

Based on the feedback from the focus group(s), determine what revisions to make in programming and website design. Consider inviting members of the focus group(s) to become reviewers throughout the season of programming. Stay in regular communication with them, asking for feedback on their experience of the website and the programming.

Step 8. Launch the Faith Formation Network

Generate ideas for promoting and introducing the faith formation network and website to members of the target audience—those active in the congregation church and those not participating in the congregation. Develop church-wide and targeted strategies for promotion.

In your promotional efforts be sure to describe how your offerings respond to something within the lives of people. Highlight the relationship between the season of programming and the particular spiritual or religious needs, interests, passions, concerns, or life issues of people. Describe the two to three benefits of participating or engaging in faith formation. Explain to people how to use the network and how to access the activities and resources.

Use as many promotional methods as you can. Consider the following ideas:

1. Ask those who are participating in church life and faith formation to invite their friends and colleagues. Ask people to use their social networks to promote the faith formation offerings.

2. Promote engagement online by connecting to (or extending from) a gathered event, program, or ministry.

3. Send email or regular e-newsletters to targeted groups (use a service like Constant Contact or Mail Chimp or Flock Note).

4. Establish a Facebook page for faith formation for network announcements, updates, stories, and photos from people engaged in faith formation.

5. Use Twitter to announce updates, events, and invite reflections from people on their experiences in the network.

6. Purchase targeted adds on Facebook and Twitter.

7. Provide ways to share experiences using blogs, Twitter, Facebook: videos, reports, photos, and so forth. Have a contest to encourage submissions and give a prize to the best photo, video, or report.

8. Have the pastor share the benefits and information about the network at Sunday worship.

9. Host information sessions after Sunday worship and other gathered programs to describe the network and how to use it.

10. Include information about the network in new member packets. Send a personalized invitation to new members.

11. Promote the network at all gathered programs and events in the church.

Be sure to find ways to communicate the stories and examples of the benefits and blessings that are coming to individuals, groups, families, and to your whole church community. Consider short videos or audio interviews of people who are engaged and then upload them to the church website and the faith formation website, as well as Facebook.

Step 9. Evaluate Programming

There are two essential times to evaluate programming: at the completion of a program or activity and at the end of a season of programming.

A *program evaluation* can be as simple as embedding an evaluation onto the website with individual programs and activities so that people can complete an evaluation as soon as the program or activity concludes. It is also easy to develop an evaluation form on SurveyMonkey (www.surveymonkey.com) and provide a link on the website to the online evaluation. SurveyMonkey compiles the results of the evaluation and produces a report of the results that can then be printed. (There are sample educational evaluation tools on SurveyMonkey that can be adapted.)

A *seasonal evaluation* reviews both programming and the website design and usability. The seasonal evaluation combines face-to-face evaluation meetings with online evaluation tools such as SurveyMonkey (www.surveymonkey.com).

For the *face-to-face seasonal evaluation*: gather small groups of people (twelve to twenty) who participated in programming and utilized the website. Conduct this activity *twice*: once to get feedback on the content of the network—what people participated in, and second for the design and usability of the faith formation network. Make a copy of the four-quadrant grid (on the next page) on newsprint or a whiteboard to capture people's feedback in four different areas. Draw a plus in the upper left quadrant, a triangle in the upper right quadrant, a question mark in the lower left quadrant, and a light bulb in the lower right quadrant.

- The upper left quadrant is for things people liked or found notable (in the programming and website).
- The upper right quadrant is for constructive criticism.
- The lower left quadrant is for questions that the experience raised in the lives of the people.
- The lower right quadrant is for ideas that the experiences spurred.

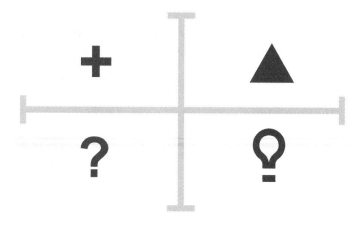

For *online seasonal evaluation*: Develop an evaluation form on SurveyMonkey (www.surveymonkey.com) and provide a link on the faith formation website and church website to the online evaluation. Design the online evaluation in two sections: an evaluation of seasonal programming and an evaluation of the website design and usability. Be sure to have people indicate if they did not participate in a program by adding a response to each question such as "did not participate." Send an email to all those who participated in one or more programs and activities in the season and ask them to go online to compete the evaluation.

Here are sample evaluation questions that can be used to construct an evaluation form or a survey instrument. For a survey, try to limit the number of essay questions. People prefer the multiple choice/rating scales. Compile the results and develop a list of areas for improvement as you plan upcoming seasons of programming.

Sample Reaction Questions

How do participants react to the program, or better, what is the measure of their satisfaction?

1. What is your overall feeling after participating in this program/activity? (*Circle all that apply.*) Enthused, Astounded, Satisfied, Indifferent, Ambivalent, Encouraged, Uneasy, Threatened, Discouraged, Affirmed, Challenged, Enriched.

2. I was pleased by/with . . .

3. I was disappointed by/with . . .

4. One thing I found most helpful in this program/activity . . .

5. One of the biggest benefits from participating in this program/activity was . . .

6. This program/activity was . . . very helpful, somewhat helpful, not very helpful, not at all helpful.

7. What recommendations would you make for improving the program?

8. Circle the number that best represents your evaluation of the program/activity. Use a rating scale of 1—strongly disagree, 2—disagree, 3—agree, and 4—strongly agree *or* a rating scale of: 1—not satisfied, 2—somewhat satisfied, 3—satisfied, 4—very satisfied, and 5—extremely satisfied.

    *   I feel that I will be able to use what I learned.
    *   The program/activity was interesting and engaging.
    *   The program/activity encouraged participation, questions, and practical application.
    *   The schedule and length of the program was appropriate.
    *   The program/activity respected my learning style.
    *   The program/activity offered a variety of learning activities and a variety of ways to learn.
    *   The program/activity helped me apply my learning to daily life.
    *   (Add specific features and content of the program/activity for people to evaluate.)

Sample Application Questions

To what extent has learning occurred? This includes understanding the content presented, changing attitudes, developing behaviors, and so forth.

1. One way I can personally use what I learned from my participation in this program/activity is . . .

2. One way this program/activity had an impact on my life . . .

3. What understandings, skills, tools, or ideas do you have now that you did not have at the beginning of the program/activity?

4. List three actions you would like to undertake as a result of your participation in the program/activity.

5. As a result of your participation in this program/activity, what do you want to learn or do next?

Step 10. Design the New Season of Programming

Using the ideas you have already generated the first time through the design process, the results from the evaluation, and the recommendations for improvement, design the new season of programming beginning at Step 4: Design a Season of Faith Formation Programming.

Works Cited

Krug, Steve. *Don't Make Me Think: A Common Sense Approach to Web Usability* (Third Edition). Berkeley: New Riders, 2014.

Syvertsen, Amy, K., Eugene C. Roehlkepartain, and Peter C. Scales. *The American Family Assets Study*. Minneapolis: Search Institute, 2012. (http://www.search-institute.org/research/family-strengths)

Worksheets

All of the worksheets in this chapter can be found online in MS Word files for easy use: www.21stCenturyFaithFormation.com.

CHAPTER 5

REIMAGINING THE RESOURCES

Curation may be a new word for many, but it has a long history. The term *curator* comes from the Latin word *curare* meaning "to care for." Every time we visit a museum we experience the work of museum curators who acquire, care for, develop, display, and interpret a collection of artifacts or works of art in order to inform, educate, and entertain us. Museum curators are subject-matter experts who guide a museum's overall art collection.

Librarians have a similar curation task—they curate books and media in a variety of forms, including digital—to inform, educate, and entertain us. Like museum curators, librarians have done this for centuries. The Library of Alexandria (Egypt) in the ancient world had curators over two thousand years ago!

Today, the concept of curation and curators has spread beyond the world of museums and libraries to all forms of digital content. In *Curation Nation*, Steven Rosenbaum writes,

> In the past we lived in a world of disciplines. The senior editorial leadership at magazines were known as editors. The folks who chose which TV shows played on a TV network were programmers. The people who picked which things would be on the shelves of your local stores were retailers. Each of these professions involved choosing the right things, putting them in the proper order, and creating a collection that was appealing to an audience or consumer. Oh, and there was that rarified individual who selected objects of art to present in a museum or gallery: they were called curators.

Today, curation is the coin of the realm. Film Festivals curate their program. Web sites curate their editorial. The team at the shopping site Gilt Group curates the items it offer for sale. *Curation* was once a word that seemed to mean highbrow, expensive, out of reach of mere mortals. But today museum curators must compete with media curation at Newser, collections of handmade crafts at Etsy, or the curated collection of the best roll-on luggage at Squidoo. Certainly curation means quality, but now quality is in the eye of the beholder (Rosenbaum, 3).

We live surrounded by an abundance of digital content. We are shifting from an era of content scarcity to one of content abundance. Daniel J. Levitan writes, "Google estimates that there are 300 exabytes (300 followed by 18 zeros) of human-made information in the world today. Only four years ago there were just 30 exabytes. We've created more information in the past few years than in all of human history before us." Here are just a few examples of the explosion of digital content (as of January 2015):

- There are between 175–200 million blogs and growing.
- There are over 700 million websites and growing.
- Over 23 million students from around the world have used the thousands of lessons and videos on The Khan Academy (https://www.khanacademy.org), for free.
- There are over 1900 Ted Talks (www.ted.com) available for free.
- There are over 400 interactive online classes and MOOCs from the world's best universities on EdX (MIT, Harvard, Berkeley, and more), and they are free.
- Over 300 hours of video are uploaded to YouTube every minute. (There are 1 billion YouTube users.)
- There have been over 20 billion photos shared on Instagram.
- And one last, mind-expanding statistic: Google estimates that there are 60 trillion web pages and growing (yes, that is trillion).

It's easy to see why so many people are overwhelmed with the explosion of digital content and its availability anytime and anywhere via mobile devices—laptops, tablets, phones, and now watches. Never has it been more important for people—curators—to sort through this vast amount of content and present it in a way that is meaningful and organized for us. This is the role of content curation. Beth Kanter describes content curation in this way,

Content curation is the process of sorting through the vast amounts of content on the web and presenting it in a meaningful and organized way around a specific theme. The work involves sifting, sorting, arranging, and publishing information. A content curator cherry picks the best content that is important and relevant to share with their community. It isn't unlike what a museum curator does to produce an exhibition: They identify the theme, they provide the context, they decide which paintings to hang on the wall, how they should be annotated, and how they should be displayed for the public.

Content curation is not about collecting links or being an information pack rat, it is more about putting them into a context with organization, annotation, and presentation. Content curators provide a customized, vetted selection of the best and most relevant resources on a very specific topic or theme. . . . A content curator continually seeks, makes sense of, and shares the best and most relevant content on a particular topic online (Beth's Blog, October 4, 2011).

A content curator is someone who continually finds, groups, organizes, and shares the best and most relevant content on a specific subject to match the needs of a specific audience. Content curators provide a personalized, high-quality selection of the best and most relevant content and resources available. They do not create more content, but make sense of all the content that others are creating. Curation is an evolving idea that addresses two parallel trends: the explosive growth in information and our need to be able to find information in coherent, reasonably contextual groupings.

One of the best ways to understand content curation is to see it in practice. Visit the following websites to see how they organize, describe, and present their content:

- NPR Music (www.npr.org/music)
- Curated Children's Books (www.curatedchildrensbooks.com)
- Edutopia (www.edutopia.org)
- The Food Network (www.foodnetwork.com)
- HGTV (www.hgtv.com)
- Faith and Leadership (www.faithandleadership.com)
- Congregational Resource Guide (http://thecrg.org)

CURATION AND FAITH FORMATION

How does curation apply to faith formation? When a faith formation curriculum was a matter of selecting the right print resource from the right religious publisher, there was little need for curation. Leaders simply selected the right resource. But even in the era of "the resource is the curriculum," many faith formation leaders were curators. To design home-grown programming they would search through print resources—and perhaps films or music—to design a retreat or a youth meeting or an adult topical series or a parent workshop. They never thought of themselves as curators, but that is what they were doing—searching through a variety of resources, selecting the most appropriate resources to match with the needs of the people and the program, and then using the resource in the program design.

We are moving to a new model of faith formation where the resource is not the curriculum. Just the opposite: the curriculum has many resources—in all types of media formats. In this new model we move from *need* to *content area* to *programming* to *resource*. Resources are essential, but they are the last step in the design process. And we will need a wide variety of resources to bring to life a curriculum that is now seen as *a lifelong journey of discipleship*—a process of experiencing, learning, and practicing the Christian faith as we seek to follow Jesus and his way in today's world.

Fortunately, we now live in a era where there is an abundance of religious content in digital form—audio, video, apps, e-books, websites—and in print form. We are benefiting from the rise of online resource centers with freely accessible, high-quality religious content and experiences that congregations, families, and individuals can access. For example, *Workingpreacher.org* from Luther Seminary has hosted 2.5 million visits from preachers in more than two hundred countries over the past twelve months (as of January 2015). The *YouVersion Bible* app—with hundreds of versions (translations) of the Bible in over a hundred languages—has been installed over 170 million times on phones and tablets. Its app for children (Bible App for Kids) has been downloaded five million times in the fourteen months since its launch in November 2013. *VibrantFaithatHome.org* has over six hundred faith-forming activities for families with children, adolescents, young adults, and adults—all available for free. And these examples can be multiplied hundreds of times.

In the new digital world of abundant resources, the role of the faith formation leader is shifting from *providing* religious content and programming to *curating* religious content and experiences for all ages. The convergence of an abundance of content, the variety of programming on a faith formation network to address the diverse needs and interests of people today, and the online platform for delivering programming and connecting people is creating the impetus for faith formation leaders to reimagine their primary role.

The abundance of available resources means that there is a need for trusted guidance in finding and selecting quality religious content and experiences. People are looking for trusted guides to select quality faith formation experiences and curate learning paths and resources to explore and learn more deeply on a specific topic. In a faith formation network people rely on curators to select the very best content to engage them in experiencing, learning, and practicing the Christian faith.

So what is a faith formation curator? **A faith formation curator is a trusted guide who continually finds, groups, organizes, and connects the best**

and most relevant content and resources on a specific subject to match the needs of a specific audience. The subjects can be one of the eight faith-forming processes, a life stage issue, a family faith practice, parenting knowledge and skills, missional programming, and more. The resources can come in many forms: people resources, programs at church and in the community, and media resources (print, audio, video, online, digital). Curation is the way that faith formation leaders connect programming with high-quality resources.

CURATING RELIGIOUS CONTENT

We can identify four primary roles in the process of curating faith formation: 1) research and organize resources, 2) identify potential resources for the curriculum, 3) evaluate resources, and 4) connect the resources to network programming. The research and organize phase of the process is continuous. Good curators are always searching for new resources and organizing them for future use.

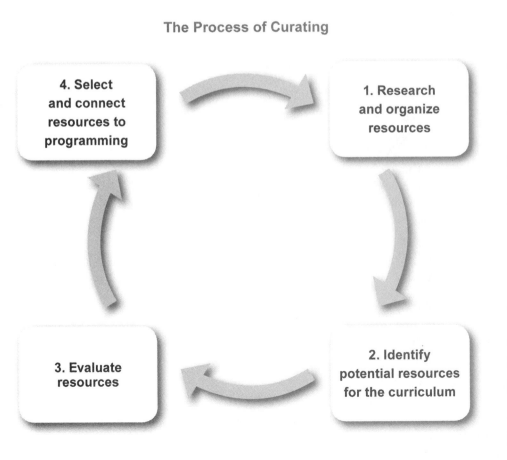

The Process of Curating

4. Select and connect resources to programming

1. Research and organize resources

3. Evaluate resources

2. Identify potential resources for the curriculum

Preparation: Build a Curation Support System

A curator relies on a support system of people, online resources, and communication to locate resources for the faith formation curriculum, and to stay up-to-date on new resources. Here are several important elements in building a curation support system and getting organized for the work of faith formation curation.

Develop trusted expert curators to assist. These people can be asked (call, text, or email) for assistance in curating resources for a particular audience or topic. We all know people in faith formation who make it part of their work to stay current with the best resources. Make a list of these people and invite them to be part of the curation support system. People who have curation in their DNA are happy to assist by recommending the best resources.

Develop a list of high-quality online resource centers. These centers should have trusted, high-quality content. Be selective—this does not have to be a long list of websites. Select resource centers with well-produced content. Review websites from national and regional denominational agencies, religious publishers, religious organizations with faith formation content, and non-profit organizations with online content for children, youth, young adults, adults, and families. There are hundreds of online resource centers with free content that can be used in matching resources to programming. Here are several websites (as of January 2015) that illustrate high-quality content that can serve as a guide for building a list of online resource centers. For more websites go to: www.CuratingFaithFormation.com.

- Bible: Enter the Bible (www.enterthebible.org)
- Church Year Resources: Loyola Press (www.loyolapress.com/liturgical-year.htm)
- Congregation: Congregational Resource Guide (http://thecrg.org)
- Family and parents: ParentFurther (www.parentfurther.com)
- Family: Catholic Family Faith (www.catholicfamilyfaith.org)
- Faith formation activities: Vibrant Faith at Home (http://vibrantfaithathome.org)
- Faith formation activities: St. Mary's Press Resource Center (www.smp.org/resourcecenter)
- Faith formation activities: Lesson Plans that Work (http://episcopaldigitalnetwork.com/lessons)
- Faith formation activities: Faith Gateway (www.faithgateway.com)
- Spirituality: Explore Faith (www.explorefaith.org)
- Spirituality: Spirituality and Practice (www.spiritualityandpractice.com)
- Worship: The Text This Week (http://www.textweek.com)
- Worship: Working Preacher (www.workingpreacher.org)

For online video resource centers go to:

- Chuck Knows Church (www.chuckknowschurch.com)
- G_dcast (www.g-dcast.com)
- Outside da Box (https://outsidedabox.com)
- The Skit Guys (http://skitguys.com)
- VCat (Video Catechism) (www.vcat.org)
- The Work of the People (www.theworkofthepeople.com)
- WorshipHouse Media (www.worshiphousemedia.com)

Subscribe to faith formation blogs and newsletters. These resources review faith formation resources to make it easier to keep up-to-date on what's new. Blogs and newsletters are produced by individuals, denominational offices, seminaries, religious organizations, and religious publishers. Here are several blogs and newsletters that illustrate faith formation curation (as of January 2015):

- Build Faith (www.buildfaith.org)
- Children's Ministry (http://childrensministry.com)
- CRC Network—Christian Reformed Church (http://network.crcna.org)
- Calvin Institute of Christian Worship (http://worship.calvin.edu)
- eCatechist (www.ecatechist.com)
- Faith & Leadership—Duke Divinity (http://faithandleadership.com)
- Key Resources—Virginia Theological Seminary (www.keyhallonline.org)

Receiving blogs and newsletters can be overwhelming, so organize them by using an RSS reader (Really Simple Syndication) that categorizes blog posts and newsletters in a separate application to make viewing easy. Here are three of the highest rated applications (as of January 2015):

- *ReadKit* for Mac & iOS (http://readkitapp.com). This is a Mac RSS reader that can organize blogs and newsletter subscriptions that can be read online or offline. Just subscribe to a blog or newsletter using the RSS reader option. It also supports other RSS and curating applications: Instapaper, Pocket, Readability, Pinboard, Delicious articles, Feedly, Fever, NewsBlur, Feedbin, and Feed Wrangler.
- *G2Reader* for PC & Android (www.g2reader.com). This is a web-based RSS feed reader that requires little more than an email and password signup. G2Reader is a tool for gathering and reading blogs and websites. Just subscribe to a blog or newsletter using the RSS reader option.
- *Feedly* for Mac, iOS, PC, and Android (https://feedly.com). Feedly is a way to organize, read, and share the content of websites all in one place. Organize blogs, news sites, podcasts and YouTube channels and access them all in one place.

Curating is a twelve-month process. Faith formation curators are always looking for resources that address the needs of their target audiences and their faith formation curricula. Use the tools previously described and the three steps that follow to stay informed on the latest resources as they become available. Be sure to join mailing lists (email or RSS feeds) for selected publishers, organizations, websites, and schools in order to receive regular updates on new resources.

Step 1. Research and Organize the Resources

The first step in the curation process is researching and reviewing resources. This is the collection phase. There's no need to select or evaluate resources at this stage— the key is to collect as many high-quality resources for faith formation in all areas and age groups. Selecting potential resources for a particular curriculum and evaluating resources comes later. Every congregation needs a "library" of resources to draw upon for programming a faith formation curriculum and network. Step 1 is a continuous process—faith formation curators are always researching and organizing resources so that they are ready to match resources with programming for a new season.

Finding Resources

Finding the right resources can sound like a daunting task, given the abundance of resources available. Here are five categories of resources to explore:

- *People resources.* Research the people resources in the church, community, church agencies, colleges and seminaries, church-related organizations, and more that can be utilized in conducting programming. Develop a list of people resources and the knowledge and skills they offer.
- *Community resources.* Research the programs and activities in the community: other churches, community agencies, religious organizations, retreat and spiritual life centers, religious camps, colleges and universities, and more. Develop a list of these organizations and the types of resources they provide. Be sure to check on their website for digital programs and activities, such as webinars and video programs.
- *Religious publisher resources.* Research the print and video resources that publishers produce and the free digital resources on their websites.
- *Online resources.* Research online resource centers that provide print content in digital form, art, music, e-books, audio podcasts, videos, webinars, small group studies, online courses, and much more. Research the variety of online faith formation content offered by colleges, universities, seminaries, and religious organizations.
- *Digital resources.* Research the increasing number of Bible apps and religious apps in the App Store (Mac and iOS) and in Google Play (Android). Also

check the religion section in Best Apps for Kids (http://bestappsforkids. com) and all of the children and family recommendations at Common Sense Media (www.commonsensemedia.org).

Research Checklist

Here is a checklist of the types of resources to research:

- People: teachers, mentors/guides, program leaders, small group leaders, guest presenters
- Community programs: churches, agencies, organizations
- Educational institutions: colleges, seminaries, educational organizations
- Retreat and spiritual life centers, monasteries
- Regional and national denominational programs, events, and websites
- Museums
- Books (with study guides)
- E-books
- Apps
- Audio podcasts
- Audio learning programs
- Videos
- Video learning programs
- Online courses
- Online activities
- Television shows
- Organizational websites
- Resource center websites

Organizing Resources

The lifelong faith formation curriculum plan template provides one organizational schema for sorting resources (see the chart in Chapter 4 on page 93). For resources that can be stored on a computer, organization can be as simple as setting up folders for each age group with ten subfolders for programming (eight faith-forming processes, missional, and life stage).

For digital content a bookmarking application is essential. Bundlr (http:// bundlr.com) has the ability to create bundles with any kind of online content: articles, photos, videos, tweets, quotes, and links. By using Bundlr's "Bundle This!" button in the web browser people can clip content while browsing the Internet. Each bundle has its own public webpage so that it can be shared freely (through its link or on social networks) or even embedded on any website. For an example of a curation website that uses Bundlr to create the links go to: www.CuratingFaith-Formation.com.

Developing Homegrown Resources

One of the easiest ways to develop a library of faith formation resources is to create homegrown resources by saving and archiving church programming. Develop a plan for recording presentations and programs at church in audio/and or video format. Think of all of the opportunities throughout the year for recording programs that can be used in other learning formats such as self-study or small group study. Consider weekly sermons, adult presentations, special events, youth events, and concerts. Develop a YouTube channel for the congregation to store and categorize all of the video recordings.

Step 2. Identify Potential Resources

Using the seasonal plan for your target audience, identify potential resources to use in implementing the programming. Take each content area and identity resources that could be used in each program in the content area. No need to select the ones you are going to use at this point. Just catalog them. Once this is done, the resources can be evaluated for inclusion in the curriculum and then published to the website.

Content Area	Program 1	Resources
	Program 2	Resources

On the next page is a simple example of matching programming ideas with resources for Lent during the January–April season. The template provides a structure for organizing the resources. Many more potential resources could be added to the ones already included.

Content Area	Program	Resources
Lent	Learning about Lent	• Video: *Ash Wednesday in 2 Minutes*—Busted Halo • Video: *Ash Wednesday*—Chuck Knows Church • Activity: "Wait, Wait, Don't Tell Me: Lent"—Vibrant Faith at Home • Article: "The Three Lent Traditions: Praying, Fasting, Almsgiving" • A 40-Day Lenten Calendar • Daily Bible readings for Lent—links to a variety of online resources
	Praying	• Lent Devotions—Luther Seminary • Prayers for each of Lent—links to a variety of online resources • Table prayers for each week of Lent—links to a variety of online resources • Stations of the Cross—Fridays at church
	Almsgiving Serving	• Church-wide service day during Lent for all ages • Study and action projects: a list of justice issues and action projects that individuals and families can adopt during Lent—links to justice organizations to learning about issues and find action projects • Collection of food and clothing for the local shelter and food bank • Bible readings on justice and service during
	Fasting	• Simple meal cookbook for Lent—a variety of menus from online sources available on the faith formation website • Friday simple meals at the church

Step 3. Evaluate Resources

All faith formation curators need standards for evaluating faith formation resources that reflect their Christian tradition and the needs of their congregation. A set of evaluation standards needs to be developed locally. Consult denominational resources for evaluating curriculum resources. Most denominations have evaluation standards for assessing educational resources or textbooks. This can serve as a basis for developing the congregation's evaluation standards. Consult Sharon Ely Pearson's criteria for curriculum resources in "Curriculum and the Ministry of Christian Education" (https://www.churchpublishing.org/media/custom/IN-Formation/EvaluatingCurriculum.pdf).

Here are ten potential categories for developing a resource evaluation checklist. Add one or more focusing questions to each category. Try to keep the checklist short so that it is easy to use. Use the evaluation criteria to review the potential resources identified in Step 2 and develop a list of resources that meet the criteria.

1. Biblical content and interpretation

2. theological content and emphasis

3. developmental appropriateness

4. ethnic-cultural appropriateness

5. inclusive of diversity

6. respect for diverse ways of learning

7. appearance and visual appeal

8. ease-of-use

9. quality of experience

10. ability to be incorporated into daily and home life

Step 4. Select the Resources and Connect to Programming

Select the best resources for the faith formation curriculum and connect them to the programming. Publish the programming to the website. Sometimes this involves a description of a program with dates and times and locations; other times it will be actual content on the website for people to experience (watch a video, read an article); and other times it will be a link to the content on another website. In each case it is important to describe the relationship between the content published on the website and the learning needs of people so they can see the connection to their spiritual or religious needs, interests, concerns, or life issues.

When publishing an activity online, be sure that permission is granted for its use. If explicit permission is not given, just write to the source to request permission. For content like YouTube videos, permission is already given to play a video on the website. The same is true when linking to a resource on another website. There is no copyright issue when there is a link to the content on someone else's website. Be sure to give proper attribution to all resources: who produced it, where it was published, a website address where it can be found, etc.

The best way to see how to connect resources to programming is by viewing websites. Review two sites that I created: http://holytrinityadults.weebly.com and http://holytrinityfamilies.weebly.com, as well as links to congregational faith formation websites at www.21stCenturyFaithFormation.com in the Case Studies section.

Continue to Research and Organize the Resources

Faith formation curators are always researching and organizing resources so that they are ready to match resources with programming for a new season. Continue to add resources to the congregational library throughout the year so there's fresh content for the faith formation curriculum.

Works Cited

Kanter, Beth. "Content Curation Primer." Beth's Blog, October 4, 2011. (http://www. bethkanter.org/content-curation-101)

King. Samuel. "A Comprehensive Guide to Content Curation." Social Barrel, September 1, 2014. (http://socialbarrel.com/guide-to-content-curation/94819)

Levitan, Daniel. "We've created more information in the past few years than in all of human history before us." The Guardian, January 19, 2015. (http://www.theguardian. com/science/2015/jan/18/daniel-j-levitin-q-and-a-organised-mind-interview)

Pearson, Sharon Ely. "Curriculum and the Ministry of Christian Education." Church Publishing. (https://www.churchpublishing.org/media/custom/IN-Formation/ EvaluatingCurriculum.pdf)

Rosenbaum, Steven. *Curation Nation: Why the Future of Content Is Context.* New York: McGraw Hill, 2011.

"REIMAGINING FAITH FORMATION" ASSESSMENT TOOL

The "Reimagining Faith Formation" Assessment Tool provides a way for your congregation to examine how it is forming faith through congregational life, family faith formation, age-group faith formation, and leadership. Rate each item on a scale from poor practice (1) to excellent practice (4). Items that receive a rating of 4 (excellent) or 3 (good) indicate areas of strength. Items that receive a 2 (adequate) or 1 (poor) indicate areas for growth. After rating each of the items, circle the items that are in need of attention and development (scores of 1 or 2) and items that your congregation wants to strengthen even if it received a score of 3 (good). This tool is available online at www.21stCenturyFaithFormation.com.

PART 1. THE CONGREGATION CREATES A FAITH-FORMING CULTURE	Practice 1=poor 4=excellent
1. **God's living presence:** People experience God's living presence in community, at worship, through study, and in service.	1 2 3 4
2. **Discipleship:** People learn who God is and come to know Jesus Christ personally; learn how to be Christian; and how to discover the meaning of the Bible for their lives.	1 2 3 4
3. **Community:** People experience a life-giving spiritual community of faith, hope, and love; characterized by hospitality, welcoming, love, and support.	1 2 3 4
4. **Worship:** People experience spiritually uplifting worship experiences that are enlightening, fulfilling, inspiring, interesting, easy to understand, and relevant in daily life.	1 2 3 4
5. **Liturgical seasons:** People experience the story of faith through the celebration of the feasts and seasons of the church year.	1 2 3 4
6. **Rituals and milestones:** People experience God's love through rituals, sacraments, and milestones that celebrate significant moments in one's life and faith journey.	1 2 3 4
7. **Prayer:** People experience the presence of God as individuals and community through prayer and spiritual disciplines/practices.	1 2 3 4
8. **Learning:** People grow in faith understanding by learning the content of the Christian tradition, reflecting upon that content, integrating it their lives, and living its meaning in the world.	1 2 3 4

	Practice 1=poor 4=excellent
9. **Moral responsibility:** People develop ethical/moral responsibility—learning about Christian perspectives on moral questions and how to apply their faith to decisions about what's right and wrong.	1 2 3 4
10. **Service & Justice:** People are engaged, locally and globally, in serving those in need, working for justice, and caring for God's creation.	1 2 3 4
11. **Intergenerational relationships:** People develop intergenerational relationships and community where the Christian faith is shared, modeled, and lived.	1 2 3 4
12. **Intergenerational faith experiences:** People are engaged in intergenerational faith experiences and activities of worship, prayer, learning, and service as an integral aspect of congregational life.	1 2 3 4
13. **Digital ministry:** People can grow in faith and discipleship through online faith-forming content and social connections on the congregation's website(s) that provides content and experiences to extend participation in congregational life and ministries into daily life.	1 2 3 4

PART 2. THE CONGREGATION EQUIPS PARENTS AND FAMILIES	Practice 1=poor 4=excellent
14. **Parental faith:** The congregation helps parents and grandparents grow in faith and discipleship, and practice a vital and informed Christian faith.	1 2 3 4
15. **Parenting for faith growth:** The congregation teaches parents and grandparents the knowledge and skills for forming faith at home: caring relationships, celebrating rituals and milestones, praying, serving, learning the Christian faith, and reading the Bible.	1 2 3 4
16. **Parenting:** The congregation equips parent and grandparents with the knowledge, skills, and confidence for parenting today, and how to develop a close, warm, and affirming parenting style that promotes religious transmission at home.	1 2 3 4
17. **Family faith experiences:** The congregation provides whole family experiences that promote growth in faith and discipleship, and teaches parents how to share faith and live faith practices at home.	1 2 3 4
18. **Family faith practices:** The congregation provides families with resources to nurture growth in Christian faith and practice at home: caring relationships, celebrating rituals and milestones, praying, serving, learning the Christian faith, and reading the Bible.	1 2 3 4
19. **Family assets:** The congregation strengthens family life by developing the assets that build strong families: nurturing family relationships, establishing family shared activities and traditions, maintaining family expectations and rules, adapting to daily challenges, and connecting to the community.	1 2 3 4
20. **Digital ministry with families:** The congregation connects with families at home through an online ministry (family website, social media) that provides social interaction and a variety of content (print, audio, video, websites) for family faith practices, parent faith formation, parenting, and family asset development.	1 2 3 4

PART 3. THE CONGREGATION EMBRACES LIFELONG FAITH GROWTH AND PRACTICE	Practice 1=poor 4=excellent
21. **Lifelong:** The congregation provides a continuity of ministry and faith formation across the whole lifecycle from children through older adults that promotes growth in Christian faith and discipleship in age-appropriate ways at each stage of life.	1 2 3 4
22. **Programming:** The congregation offers a variety of age-specific experiences, programs, activities, resources, and social connections for every stage of life that are available anytime and anywhere, in physical places and online spaces, and conducted in variety of settings—self-directed, mentored, at home, in small groups, in large groups, church-wide, in the community, and in the world.	1 2 3 4
23. **Online:** The congregation uses its own website(s) as an integral component of age-group ministry and faith formation that extends gathered ministries/programs through online content (print, audio, video) and experiences, blends online and gathered activities in individual programs, and offers online-only programs, activities, and resources—all of which are available anytime, anywhere.	1 2 3 4
24. **Children:** The congregation addresses the unique life tasks, needs, interests, and religious/spiritual journeys of children through a variety of faith-forming experiences and activities focused on developing caring relationships, celebrating the liturgical seasons, celebrating rituals and milestones, learning the Christian tradition and apply it to life, praying, reading the Bible, serving /working for justice/caring for creation, and worshipping God with the faith community.	1 2 3 4
25. **Youth:** The congregation addresses the unique life tasks, needs, interests, and religious/spiritual journeys of youth through a variety of faith-forming experiences and activities focused on developing caring relationships, celebrating the liturgical seasons, celebrating rituals and milestones, learning the Christian tradition and apply it to life, praying, reading the Bible, serving /working for justice/caring for creation, and worshipping God with the faith community.	1 2 3 4
26. **Young adults:** The congregation addresses the unique life tasks, needs, interests, and religious/spiritual journeys of young adults through a variety of faith-forming experiences and activities focused on developing caring relationships, celebrating the liturgical seasons, celebrating rituals and milestones, learning the Christian tradition and apply it to life, praying, reading the Bible, serving /working for justice/caring for creation, and worshipping God with the faith community.	1 2 3 4
27. **Adults:** The congregation addresses the unique life tasks, needs, interests, and religious/spiritual journeys of adults through a variety of faith-forming experiences and activities focused on developing caring relationships, celebrating the liturgical seasons, celebrating rituals and milestones, learning the Christian tradition and apply it to life, praying, reading the Bible, serving /working for justice/caring for creation, and worshipping God with the faith community.	1 2 3 4

PART 4. THE CONGREGATION HAS FAITHFUL, COMPETENT LEADERSHIP	Practice 1=poor 4=excellent
28. **Spiritual influence:** The pastor and ministry leaders know and model the transforming presence of God in their lives and ministries.	1 2 3 4
29. **Interpersonal competence:** The pastor and ministry leaders build relationships and community in the congregation, as well as in their ministries and programs.	1 2 3 4
30. **Competent leadership:** The pastor and ministry leaders demonstrate effective leadership by modeling the way—aligning values and actions, inspiring a shared vision, challenging the process—being innovative and experimenting, enabling others to act, and encouraging the heart of others—affirming and celebrating contributions.	1 2 3 4
31. **Competent ministry:** The pastor and ministry leaders reflect superior theological, theoretical, and practical knowledge and skill for leadership in the congregation and their ministries.	1 2 3 4
32. **Volunteer leadership:** The pastor and ministry leaders nurture the faith and theological knowledge of volunteer leaders, equip them with knowledge and skills for their ministry, and provide continuing support and mentoring.	1 2 3 4

Research References

Many of the items on the "Assessment Tool" are drawn from research studies.

Items 1–4, 7, 9, 10, 14, 18, 28-29, 31–32—From *The Spirit and Culture of Youth Ministry* (The Study of Exemplary Congregations in Youth Ministry). Roland Martinson, Wes Black, and John Roberto. St. Paul, MN: EYM Publications, 2010.

Items 14–18—From *Families and Faith: How Religion Is Passed Down across Generations.* Vern Bengtson with Norella M. Putney and Susan Harris. New York: Oxford University Press, 2013.

Items 1–12—From *Generations Together: Caring, Praying, Learning, Celebrating, and Serving Faithfully.* Kathie Amidei, Jim Merhaut, and John Roberto. Naugatuck, CT: LifelongFaith Associates, 2014.

Item 19—From: *The American Family Assets Study.* Amy K. Syvertsen, Eugene C. Roehlkepartain, and Peter C. Scales. Minneapolis: Search Institute, 2012. (http://www.search-institute.org/research/family-strengths)

Items 3–10, 14–18—From "Biblical and Theological Perspectives and Best Practices for Faith Formation." Marcia Bunge. *Understanding Children's Spirituality.* Edited by Kevin Lawson. Eugene, OR: Cascade Books, 2012.

Items 14–18—"How Highly Religious Families Strive to Fulfill Sacred Purposes." David Dollahite and Loren Marks. *Sourcebook on Family Theories and Methods.* Edited by V. Bengston, D. Klein, A. Acock, K. Allen, and P. Dilworth-Anderson. Thousand Oaks, CA: Sage Publications, 2005.

Items 16 and 19—"What Makes a Good Parent?: A Scientific Analysis Ranks the 10 Most Effective Child-Rearing Practices." Robert Epstein. *Scientific American Mind*, November/December 2010.

Items 30—*The Leadership Challenge.* Fifth Edition. James M. Kouzes and Barry Z. Posner. San Francisco: Jossey-Bass, 2012.

REIMAGINING FAITH FORMATION—ONLINE RESOURCES

21st Century Faith Formation website
http://www.21stCenturyFaithFormation.com
This online resource center helps leaders design faith formation guided by the vision and practices in *Reimagining Faith Formation for the 21st Century*. This is a "how-to" resource with lots of practical tools to apply the concepts in the book, including:
- Curriculum models and strategies for faith formation with age groups, families, and all generations
- Tools and worksheets for designing faith formation curriculum
- Website design tools
- Congregational case studies
- Digital media methods and interactive tools

Curating Faith Formation website
http://www.CuratingFaithFormation.com
The Curating Faith Formation website provides links to digital content to use in designing curriculum and building a faith formation website for children, adolescents, adults, families, and all generations.

Intergenerational Faith website
http://www.IntergenerationalFaith.com
The Intergenerational Faith website is designed to extend and deepen the content in the *Generations Together* book by providing research on intergenerational religious transmission and faith formation, articles on the principles and practices of intergenerational faith formation and ministry, case studies, and book resources.

Lifelong Faith website
http://www.LifelongFaith.com
This is the main website for information and news about LifelongFaith Associates. All of the Lifelong Faith journals are available online for download. Join the mailing list by visiting the website.

Faith Formation Learning Exchange (sponsored by Vibrant Faith)
http://www.faithformationlearningexchange.net
The Faith Formation Learning Exchange provides a variety of resources—research studies, effective practices, cutting-edge thinking, real-world models and tools, and the latest resources—to help leaders develop Christian lifelong faith formation for all ages and generations.